Design for Dasein

Understanding the Design of Experiences

Thomas Wendt

For information about the author, please visit surroundingsignifiers.com

Acknowledgements

I'd like to thank my wife, Niki English, for supporting me throughout the writing process. Thanks for being there for the "I finished a chapter!" moments and the "this book is shit, I'm throwing it out!" moments, and everywhere in between.

The following people have also supported me in many ways—sometimes directly through textual feedback and idea generation, other times indirectly through me encountering their work or just asking how the book is coming along: Jenni Lee-Winter, Cameron Tonkinwise, Jeff Sussna, Martin Hensel, Stephane Vial, David Rubeli, Mark Badger, Piero Rivizzigno, Jabe Bloom, Will Evans, Peter Morville, Abby Covert, Dan Klyn, Andrew Hinton, Grant Wythoff, Phillip Hunter, Roz Duffy, Josh Tyson, Carl Nelson, Donna Lichaw, Jorge Arango, David Holl, Yana Kuchirko, Fredrik Matheson, Marsha Haverty, Simon Norris, Evan Selinger, and Klaus Krippendorff.

Contents

Chapter 1
Introduction

Embodied Philosophy

Design involves doing philosophy with the hands. This statement paraphrases an introduction Allan Chochinov gave for Cameron Tonkinwise at a small presentation in New York City. Allan mentioned that Cameron came from a background in philosophy before studying design, and explained that design is simply "doing philosophy with your hands." With that phrase, the impetus for my interest in the intersection between phenomenology and design—which I had been struggling to clearly articulate for some time—suddenly became clear. Design involves the enacting of theory through the body. This act of embodiment will be an overarching theme in this book: how we come to "do philosophy" through design, and how this activity relates to the design of experiences.

Out of all the fields that influence experience design, philosophy is one not frequently discussed. Volumes have been written on the roots of experience design within psychology, cognitive science, and anthropology, yet very little has been dedicated to philosophy, critical theory, and literary studies. Why? Perhaps it is because these latter fields are often relegated to the humanities, and are therefore perceived as less "practical." Or perhaps it is because experience design is still a young field, and we simply haven't had the time. Regardless of the reason, I believe now is the time to consider contributions from philosophy as a serious inquiry in experience design. As we see a distinct movement toward this type of inquiry in the last few years—with critical and speculative design, service design, ontological design, design thinking, and systemic design becoming more solidified as practices—my hope is for this book to contribute to the overall trend of adding rigor to experience design practice.

The focus here is on the philosophical tradition of phenomenology—specifically on its evolution through a few key phases— and its application to experience design and its offshoots. Although I started publicly speaking and writing about this topic at conferences and for design publications about a year before beginning this book, my research goes back to my undergraduate years. Each time I give a presentation, a small group of audience members will approach me afterward about how they have thought of the connection before, have not thought of it but want to learn more, or simply realize how their liberal arts degree now seems relevant. I speak about the topic with my students, and many of them end up finding a new use for their literary backgrounds. Reactions like these tell me that there are others with latent interest in the theoretical aspects of experience design; that others in the experience design community find value beyond recipe books, case studies, and the often decontextualized "best practices."

This text is born in part out of a growing dissatisfaction with the state of design theory with respect to academia and industry. Even the simple act of reading the term "design theory" likely calls up notions of academia as detached from everyday design, esoteric conversations about the nature of design, and researchers who exist outside the bounds of design practice. At least in the United States, academics and practitioners are mostly closed off from one another despite the crossover in their work. One of my goals for this text is to articulate how that gap may be bridged through rethinking the dualism of theory and practice. Phenomenology provides an excellent way to do that: instead of reaffirming the traditional binaries of theory/practice and academia/practice, we are able to discuss both at the same time as part of the same system.

The tone of the book might feel more like an academic text than a practitioner's manual. That being said, phenomenology is a framework that emphasizes praxis as a means of knowledge and understanding. This involves using theoretical frameworks to influence practical outputs, as well as using practice to influence theory. Similarly, the following examination over the next few hundred pages will aim to illustrate new ways to think about design, and hopefully inspire new practices. But this is not a recipe book—it has nothing to say about step-by-step instructions on how to perform certain design activities, or about illusory "best practices" on how to handle certain problems. Instead, it will provide the beginnings of a framework that readers can interpret for themselves. There is a difference between the purposefully obscure versus the use of language that reflects the complexity of the material. This book will do the latter. When dealing with philosophical text—especially when some of it has been translated from its original language—it is difficult to strike a balance between "plain" language and precision. The aim here is to provide both a rigorous theoretical framework and the beginnings of a practical methodology for how to embody philosophy through design.

Ship or Die

In a 2006 interview, Tim Berners-Lee referred to a new breed of Web architects as "philosophical engineers."[1] Halpin, Clark, and Wheeler associate this title with the recognition of a new iteration of the Web, which calls for a deeper understanding of its relationship to the body and mind of the user.[2] This is essentially a philosophical question. Berners-Lee was probably ahead of his time (yet again) in referring to the philosophical engineer in the light of the semantic Web. Eight years later, we're not even talking about the Web in the same way as before—we're talking about mobile and wearable devices; about networks of connected things and ecosystems of products. So far, we've done an excellent job of developing products, but a terrible job of *designing* products. That is, we've swung the pendulum too far from "thinking" to "making," which is resulting in masses of products lacking utility or potential for meaningful interaction—from internet-connected refrigerators; to dog collars that track movement from doggie bed to fire hydrant, and back; to mobile apps that simply function as digital poking devices.

The irony is that trends like the Internet of Things and wearable computing actually have potential to introduce completely new interactions and experiences into our current conception of computing. These areas are the domains of the philosophical engineer. But startup economies and venture capital firms have emphasized speed to market and returns on investment, to the point where "the launch" has become a fetishized event. Products are "designed" in a matter of weeks, even days. They are isolated from the entire product's landscape and designed in a vacuum—polished but not architected, beautiful but useless, conceptually unique but aesthetically templated, commercially viable but morally corrupt. While this is not to say design should be a long drawn-out process, it certainly should not be an afterthought. We need to take the time to understand the nature of problems and user needs, the implications of our design decisions, and how design executions manifest themselves in the world.

My hypothesis for why we are designing products at such a rapid rate is multifaceted. First, I should note that I am speaking within an American context, in which venture capital firms seem to be throwing money at any consumer product that comes along. This has created an environment of competition for funds much in the same way corporate products compete for market share. The difference within startup economies is that instead of only launching "on brand" products, there is a large benefit to being fast/first to market. Ironically, this obsessive need to launch and iterate is precisely what links design to phenomenology; the emphasis on praxis and time spent testing with users is a phenomenological concern. But we will save that for later.

Startups have fostered a large amount of backlash against the academic side of design research. Asking a 23-year-old startup founder to spend a month understanding who his end users are—what frustrates them, what their lives look like, why they would ever use his product—is like asking to throw away 30+ days of development time. Movements like Lean Startup and Lean User Experience have done an excellent job of emphasizing the importance of customer insight. And yet, they are easily bastardized into biased methods that end up reinforcing the shallow assumptions they set out to eradicate. On the other end of the spectrum, academic design research is often perceived as esoteric and disconnected from design practice.

The origin of this difference between academia and industry is associated with a paradox found within design—a paradox I think phenomenology can help explain and solve. This book will dedicate an entire chapter to articulating what I'm calling the "problem-solution paradox," which states that problems and solutions evolve together and must be understood together. There will be much more to say about this later, but for now, we might say that treating design problems and solutions as a linear movement (from problem to solution) creates an unnecessary distinction and a false assumption about "where to start." This is where academics and industry professionals get tripped up. One goal of this book is to use phenomenology to reframe the ways we think about problems and solutions. If we can better understand how problems and solutions manifest themselves, we are in a better position to articulate an understanding of design that doesn't fall into this binary trap.

Phenomenological Design Thinking

Approaching design from a phenomenological perspective will accomplish a few things: 1) it allows us to talk about how a phenomenological groundwork influences design theory and practice; 2) it pushes the evolution of phenomenology to its logical conclusion, from a focus on Being to technology to design; and 3) it allows us to formulate a design process that combines both speed and rigor.

Phenomenology has been through a few important evolutions. Though one can argue that it traces back to the ancient Greeks, our focus begins thousands of years later. Beginning with Edmund Husserl's formulations of individual experience with the world, Husserl's student Martin Heidegger broke quite radically from his tutelage and expanded phenomenology into the study of being. Around the same time, Maurice Merleau-Ponty was rethinking phenomenology from the perspective of embodiment, prioritizing bodily experience over theoretical reflection. Contemporary philosophers—such as Done Ihde, Peter-Paul Verbeek, and others who I will cite frequently in the coming pages—have focused on Heidegger's interest in technology and Merleau-Ponty's interest in the body, rethinking phenomenology yet again as post-phenomenology. This new movement highlights the role of technological objects as the source of insight about the world and our relationship to it (or even if "we" are separate from "it"), along with how embodiment can explain our involvement with tasks, goals, and other people.

While the history of phenomenology is not our focus here, this short introduction should point to the idea that the next stage of this evolution is design-centric. If technology is a means of understanding the world, then how we design technology becomes massively important. In a certain sense, we cannot talk about technology without talking about design. In turn, I am proposing that the next evolution of phenomenology is a sort of phenomenological design thinking. This approach gives post-phenomenology a more purposeful tone, explaining not only *why* technology is important but also *how* we can design it. It also provides a new perspective on design thinking—a topic that seems to have fallen out of style in the past few years, but still, I believe, provides excellent theory for designers to put into practice.

Nigel Cross explains three facets of design research:

- design epistemology – study of designerly ways of knowing
- design praxiology – study of the practices and processes of design
- design phenomenology – study of the form and configuration of artefacts[3]

While I understand his desire to break these fields apart and define them independently, I want to argue that design phenomenology as defined here is too narrow in focus (and it actually encompasses the other two). With a phenomenological approach to design, we can talk about how design thinking would include what Cross calls "design praxiology," as the knowledge of artifacts is dependent on how we design and use those artifacts. And, if those artifacts embody our understanding of the world, they will then always include a sense of design epistemology.

I will attempt to articulate how philosophy is enacted through design, and how the coming-together of design and philosophy contributes to each field. We are at a time in phenomenology when the current formulations need to take action; we need a plan for how to implement this type of thinking about the world within the world. And, we are at a time in design when we need strong theoretical foundations on which to build future practice. I hope that the critical analysis in this book will contribute to that.

A Note on Experience Design

The idea that experience design is an ambiguous, often confused field will probably be no surprise to most readers. Practitioners spend countless hours debating what experience design is, what kinds of design practices it includes, and whether it should even be considered a design discipline. For the purposes of this text, we will ignore that mostly unproductive debate. Instead, let us assume that experience design is a blanket term describing the collective activities of multiple design practices including, but not limited to, design research, interaction design, visual design, industrial design, interface design, (information) architecture, and many more. It is concerned with the cumulative experiential qualities a user might have with a system, and therefore has its roots in psychology, cognitive sciences, anthropology, sociology, and philosophy, among others. In many cases, an experience designer may follow multiple design practices with varying levels of expertise in each.

The first question one might ask is whether *designing an experience* is really possible. This is a very valid question, and one that we will return to throughout this book. Before answering it, we should consider the origins of design as a uniquely modern practice: "There is no word in classical Hebrew or Greek that translates our word 'design'. This etymological fact immediately reinforces the idea that there is indeed something peculiarly modern about design, that design may be indicative of a way of being-in-the-world that is distinctive of the modern historical period."[4] Mitcham points out that design, as we currently know it, emerged out of the modern period as differentiated from previous craft-based societies. Craft was characterized by the lack of separation between the one creating the object and the one using it. That is, craftspeople created objects for themselves. Consider an artist: more often than not, the artist crafts artwork according to their individual aesthetic with the purpose of communicating how they themselves see the world. Now compare the artist's craft to the work of an interaction designer. Though also creating a system with their personal aesthetic, the interaction designer is constrained by industry standards and market viability, as well as concerned with end user's behavioral patterns and technological feasibility. Mitcham calls our attention to the peripheral aspects of creation that signify a crafted object over a designed object, with the latter being the result of a complex system of influences on how the object might take shape.

The various etymological roots of design that Mitcham highlights all point to a purposeful act or intentional plan that designers execute in the design process. We get the sense that design is the purposeful enacting of a plan, whereas craft might account for and embrace a more open process. A product of the artistic process should be open to the user's interpretation and will mean different things for different users, while the product of the interaction design process—though it will always contain interpretive aspects—should communicate meaning in a more structured way. The interaction designer must assert some kind of control over the use of the object, usually through things like strong information architecture, explicit affordances, and clear instruction. But all of these things have to do with specific elements of the interface, not necessarily the experience. We will return to these ideas, along with counterpoints, throughout the book.

This point is crucial to understanding experience design. There is a key difference between a product or service, and the *experience of* that product or service. Surely, we cannot dictate the experience, as it is a purely personal phenomenon. Experience is based on unique interpretation and is often vastly different across individuals. But while we might not be able to dictate experience, we can certainly design for the potential of certain qualitative experiences over others. Think of the last time you went to a retail store. What kind of music was playing? How did it smell? What was the temperament of the employees? How was merchandise laid out? These are all designed aspects of the store that influenced your interpretation of it. There is a massive experiential difference in a retail store playing light rock versus hip hop versus black metal. Similarly, there is an experiential difference between workers trained for efficiency, as they are in Starbucks, versus workers trained for exclusivity, such as a doorman at a private club. Each example represents the purposeful, hopeful design of a certain outcome. Of course, we cannot create one-to-one causal relationships between store environment and customer experience, but we can certainly make choices that might lead to desired outcomes—e.g., light rock music will likely make shoppers feel more relaxed than black metal.

Mitcham also calls our attention to the rift between designers and users, which allows us to reframe our focus on experience. Experience design is an inherently fickle endeavor; our inability to create causal relationships between users and their designed environments forces us to take a broad view of experience design—understanding it as the emergent effects of many design practices, rather than a practice in itself. An experience designer might design interactions, objects, interfaces, services, products, none of these, or all of these. What emerges out of their interactions with one another, and with a user, is an experience. The design of experiences, then, is an inherently multi-disciplinary and trans-disciplinary practice, involving fields of expertise from both inside and outside of design.

A Note on the Text

The difficulty with talking about phenomenology is always associated with terminology. Much of its history is wrapped up in Martin Heidegger's work—a major figure in philosophy who contributed to many of our conceptions of the world. He is also known for his embracing of the complexities of his native German language. As with any translation, English versions of his texts are packed with footnotes explaining linguistic nuances and word choices, leaving English readers with a sense of unnecessary complexity. Writing on these topics places an author in a difficult position: they can either embrace the strange translations we have, or develop new words and risk a discontinuity between texts. I will attempt to stay consistent with popular translations without being unnecessarily complex in language, and will offer explanation when needed.

This text walks a strange line between academia and practice, with all the baggage that comes on both sides. At various points, it will serve as an exegesis of the intersection of design and phenomenology, a critique of phenomenology, or a critique of experience design. I will provide short accounts of the history of phenomenology when necessary so as not to go too far off topic. At its core, this text is a survey of a very large landscape.

Many readers will notice that I tend to use a lot of quotes. These are meant to serve both as reference points for the arguments I am attempting to make, and to give the reader sufficient background. One aspect of many design texts that is missing from this one is case studies, except for the occasional reference to a project. There are a few reasons behind this: 1) Case studies are often quite boring, quickly outdated, and often decontextualized. I believe there is more value in strong frameworks than in accounts of single instances, at least for the current purposes. 2) I do not believe that every claim within design needs to be backed-up with cases. Some of the concepts we will deal with in this book are emergent; they have not been explicitly considered until now. That is not to say anything here is revolutionary or that it does not help explain current work. The issue, I believe, is that designers have become much too reliant on case studies, recipe books, and step-by-step guides that are decontextualized from the individual designer. This book will provide none of those. Instead, it will attempt to introduce a different way of thinking about experience design that the reader can adapt to their own situation.

Chapter 2
Phenomenology and Experience Design

Dasein is a Design Process

"Every Dasein is styled through the consumption of design. Without design, Dasein is meaningless."[5]

Martin Heidegger produced a significant shift from what we might think of as traditional phenomenology espoused by his teacher, Edmund Husserl. Heidegger claimed that philosophy has historically been too focused on theoretical formulations, and not concerned enough with the everyday interactions of bodily entities. He aimed to bring philosophy down from the lofty heights of Plato's forms, Descartes' dualism, and Husserl's maintenance of the subject-object split. Heidegger's criticism of these previous thinkers is mainly that they failed to concern themselves with Being, positing that "The question of the meaning of Being is the most universal and the emptiest of questions."[6] In this sense, Heidegger's work attempts to articulate the philosophy of Being as a philosophy of the everyday; he is more concerned with everyday practice than with theoretical models. The emptiness of Heidegger's question can be felt in its apparent paradox. Heidegger attempts to mundane-ify philosophy, but he does so by asking the most general and wide-ranging question he possibly can: the question of Being as it relates to the hermeneutical reading of the world through interactions with things. Most of this chapter will consist of summarizing Heidegger's core thinking in relation to experience design, and to introduce topics we will return to later.

The most crucial, wide ranging, and complex notion within Heidegger's work is that of Dasein. Broken into its individual parts, the German word *Da* (here/there) is combined with *Sein* (being) to result in a literal translation of here/there-being, or sometimes called being-there or being-in-the-world. Dasein is situated Being, not as an abstract form or overarching concept that might explain our current embodied state, but rather it *is* our embodied state. Our everyday experience of the world is what characterizes our conception of Being, as opposed to strict duality between thinking and doing. The preservation of the German word Dasein in most English translations and secondary literature (including this one) illustrates the importance of maintaining the sense of situated-ness of Being. We cannot talk about Being in terms of consciousness separated from an agent's particular spatial, temporal, and contextual mode of being, as many prior philosophers who Heidegger critiques have done (most notably, René Descartes, who will be discussed in the next section).

Heidegger notes that "Dasein exists as a being for which, in its being, that being is itself an issue."[7] Self-consciousness is a necessary characteristic of Dasein, as the being needs to be conscious of and concerned with its own Being. That ability for humans to reflectively look back, analyze, and experience anxiety over their current situation is what makes Dasein distinct from other modes of being. A plant might have a mode of being, but it lacks the ability to be concerned with itself as a being; in Heidegger's conceptualization, the plant does not possess Dasein. In fact, it turns out only humans and perhaps some higher primates can be thought of as Dasein. We are the only species capable of becoming so wrapped up in our everyday, mundane experience to the point where the resulting anxiety pervades every moment of existence.

Dasein's central characteristic is the situated-ness of Being, illustrated by the *Da* (here/there). Dasein is the Being to which we can point and say "that one." It is "in," as being-in-the-world. But we should be careful when interpreting "in" as a spatial relationship:

> Heidegger holds that human beings (which he refers to as Dasein) and world are not two distinct entities but only one which results from Dasein's involvement in the world. Thus the in of being-in-the-world is unrelated to ideas of Aristotelian containment, instead in is better understood in terms of involvement. Heidegger characterises everyday life as being an engaged, absorbed involvement in an undifferentiated world.[8]

In order to understand "in" in this context, we need to step away from ideas of spatiality and physical proximity. Being-in refers primarily to being-involved in a particular situation. This point is especially important for designers. When considering user context, it is easy to fall back on location as the primary contextual information. Our language is filled with metaphors of space,[9] and theories on designing for context have relied on location as a primary driver for a long time. For example, when we design an experience for air travel it is easy to become caught up in considering physical locations: cab to the airport, airport terminal, lounge, bar, security, on the plane, etc. The difficult part, however, is to understand the user's *involvement* with each of those locations in relation to their concern. When in a security line, the concern is certainly with physical surroundings, but also with the tasks to be done (remove liquids, take off shoes, etc.), authority, process, time until takeoff, etc. The post-security mindset is often quite different in that although the user is in a very similar physical location, there are now different concerns: getting to the gate, finding food before boarding, making a call, finding a power outlet, etc. The notion of being-in-the-world has different meanings at different times, and is affected by more than spatial location.

Another reason to interpret "in" as *involved*—instead of or in addition to a spatial relationship—is that Heidegger attempted to articulate Dasein and the world as undifferentiated. There is no separation between self and world, as we see in Cartesian philosophy and subsequent cognitive science. There is no mind/body problem for Heidegger, as body and mind are both inherently linked to the world via engaged interaction with it. Or as Paul Dourish states, "Instead of asking, 'How can we know about the world?' Heidegger asked, 'How does the world reveal itself to us through our encounters with it?'"[10] The world exposes or reveals itself only when Dasein manipulates it; through interactions with things, we come to know about ourselves and our surroundings. Our goal as designers, then, is to understand how users interpret their own involvement with the world as a meaningful activity. We are interested in what actions users take and how those actions result in meaning formation—though, too often, design research has focused on the former but not the latter. Budgets and client expectations force researchers to hyper-focus on actions taken over meaning derived, as actions can easily be considered "more real" and more commercially viable. Yet, without deriving meaning from interactions, the actions themselves are simply pantomime.

Heidegger's main text, *Being and Time*, offers a vision of Being as something always ahead of itself. That is, Heidegger questions the concept of "now," asserting instead that all current focus is directed toward the future. We are constantly taking action toward a future goal, and that goal is what drives Being—we eat in order to sustain ourselves and to enjoy the taste of food; we work in order to obtain money and feel a sense of satisfaction; we seek friendship in order to feel connected to others; etc. The implications for design are self-evident: everything we design should have the end user's future goals in mind. Designers have come to terms with the idea that users are interacting with a product or service not for the sake of simply interacting, but rather in order to accomplish something else—something less tangible. This is the essence of time for Dasein: it is always ahead of itself or behind itself. Or as Stiegler puts it: "Dasein is in the mode of 'having-to-be' because it never yet totally is; inasmuch as it exists, it is never finished, it always already anticipates itself in the mode of 'not yet.' Between birth and death, existence is what extends itself [Erstreckung] between 'already' and 'not yet.'"[11] This idea of Dasein as a temporally situated entity has been translated directly into the design process through research methods and ideation—the former to understand the past and present, and the latter to anticipate the future through the perceived goal-orientation of Dasein. Designers use induction and deduction to understand the present state of a user's world, and use that insight to abductively create alternate futures.

Being and Time also characterizes Dasein as being "thrown." That is, Dasein is dropped into a world with which it must cope. Our contextual situation is almost never ideal, so we cope with it. We can think about coping as dealing with broken things, but also as the simple way of incorporating things into our everyday lives. This type of incorporation necessitates design:

> Authentic Dasein is an unceasing attempt to give a decisive turn to our state of thrownness in the world by moving together to design a society. Design, then, equates to making decision about form in order to liberate us from the arbitrariness of life. Paraphrasing Nietzsche, we can see this as a throw of the dice on the table of the gods. We must ost-werpen our lives [the Dutch word for 'design' can also be read as 'un-throw' - Tr]. The etymology refers to making order out of chaos. The English word *design* also

contains echoes of sketching and marking out. Thrownness-unthrowing: there you have the human condition.[12]

The somewhat bleak picture that Heidegger paints of everyday existence as "thrown" is mitigated by design. As we move through everyday life, we change things in our environment—from small changes such as turning the heat up in our home, to large changes such as transitioning to a new job. In this way, we assert control over our place within the environment; we redesign the current state to better meet our needs. We un-throw ourselves (thanks to the wonders of the Dutch language) in order to find a home. The act of coping is not simply sacrificing—it is a movement, intentional or unintentional, toward a more preferable state.[13]

This altering from non-preferable to preferable is what links design to Dasein: "Dasein has no clothes, no habitat, no biology, no hormones, no atmosphere around it, no medication, no viable transportation system even to reach his Hütte in the Black Forest. Dasein is thrown into the world but is so naked that it doesn't stand much chance of survival."[14] Dasein is a sort of situated blank slate—it comes into the world without influence, and exists according to the capacity of the body. In a sense, Dasein is both omnipotent and completely powerless—omnipotent because our entire existence is predicated on the idea of situatedness and embodiment, and powerless because Dasein is completely dependent on bodies and objects. Dasein's "survival" depends on the bodies and things it encounters.

The relationship between Dasein and its objects will be a common theme throughout this book, but for a preliminary illustration I would like to turn to the novel *Malone Dies* by Samuel Beckett. Beckett's literature is characterized by a nonlinear, minimalist but often-repetitive prose depicting the extreme mundane nature of everyday life, stripped down to its core. In *Malone Dies*, Beckett describes a bed-ridden man in a dark room. He is unsure of where he is or how he got there; all he knows are the objects around him, which he cherishes as the only parts of his life left with any meaning. These objects include things like a pencil, a chamber pot, dishes, and a long stick used as an extension of his arm to bring distant objects closer. Malone's ambivalent relationship with his objects often results in childish lament and acting out: "What a misfortune, the pencil must have slipped from my fingers, for I have only just succeeded in recovering it after forty-eight hours of intermittent efforts. What my stick lacks is a little prehensile proboscis like the nocturnal tapir's. I should really lose my pencil more often, it might do me good, I might be more cheerful, it might be more cheerful."[15] Malone lives in a completely bare existence—a literary method Beckett uses to focus the reader on the most minute aspects of the scene. In this passage, Malone laments the loss of his pencil, which he only finds after two days of rummaging around his bed sheets. Once he finds the pencil, Malone expresses ambivalence toward the pencil and his stick, which he deems inadequate.

In another passage, Malone ponders his stick as a means of accomplishment only after he loses it:

> It is a disaster. I suppose the wisest thing now is to live it over again, meditate upon it and be edified. [...] Now that I have lost my stick I realize what it is I have lost and all it meant to me. And thence ascend, painfully, to an understanding of the Stick, shorn of all its accidents, such as I have never dreamt of. What a broadening of the mind. So that I half discern, in the veritable catastrophe that has befallen me, a blessing in disguise [...] I thought I was turning my stick to the best possible account, like a monkey scratching its fleas with the key that opens its cage.[16]

Malone is a simplistic example of Dasein as being-involved in objects. Throughout the novel, Malone's stick is treated both as a friend and as a means of attaining other objects. He uses it to grab hold of his food cart, to rearrange his sheets, and to find lost objects.

> The door half opens, a hand puts a dish on the little table left there for that purpose, takes away the dish of the previous day, and the door closes again. This is done for me every day, at the same time probably. When I want to eat I hook the table with my stick and draw it to me. It is on castors, it comes squeaking and lurching towards me. When I need it no longer I send it back to its place by the door. It is soup. They must know I am toothless. I eat it one time out of two, out of three, on an average. When my chamber-pot is full I put it on the table, beside the dish. Then I go twenty-four hours without a pot. No, I have two pots. They have thought of everything.[17]

Everything in Malone's life is taken care of for him either by objects or by other people. Still, he cherishes objects like the stick and the pencil because they allow him to alter his conditions, and might even provide the means of radical improvement ("like a monkey scratching its fleas with the key that opens its cage") if only he can become aware of their full capabilities. Completely stripped of all creative capacities, Dasein plays itself out in Malone through the seemingly trivial objects with which he interacts. Without those object, he is docile and heartbroken.

Malone is meant to be an extreme example. But still, on a certain level, any reader can see similarities between themselves and Malone. We cherish objects in much the same way, as these objects are our only way of playing out Dasein via designing situations for ourselves. A prime example is the mobile device. If you have ever forgotten your phone at home, you can likely relate to the sense of loss felt without that object. This is not simply because the phone has become a fetishized consumer object, but also because the phone provides an almost infinite means of interactions that allow the user to attain goals. Without that cluster of affordances we call a mobile device, we are forced to design our situations by other means that seem substandard in comparison. We are all like Malone. Our objects define us. They shape our understanding of the world.

Connecting the Poles of Self and World

The stress that phenomenology places on things is wrapped up in its rejection of Cartesian dualism. René Descartes was a philosopher whose work shaped centuries of psychology, cognitive science, and "common sense" ways of knowing the world and ourselves. Descartes became foundational in rational philosophy when he asserted his famous dictum: "cogito ergo sum." This amazingly pithy phrase—"I think, therefore I am"—attempts to encapsulate that which we cannot doubt. Through painstaking introspection, Descartes was ostensibly able to logically conclude that everything can be doubted except for the process of thinking. If he thinks, he exists. The activity of the mind became the groundwork for any and all future conclusions.

Recent work on embodied, situated, and distributed cognition has challenged Descartes' conclusion, and will be discussed later. For our present purposes, it is important to note that the *Cogito* places the activity of the mind over that of the body. The mind is an executive function, and the body is simply a bag of meat that follows orders. Descartes articulates a theory of mind based wholly on the intangible properties of the mind as separate from the body: "I thence concluded that I was a substance whose whole essence or nature consists only in thinking, and which, that it may exist, has need of no place, nor is dependent on any material thing; so that 'I,' that is to say, the mind by which I am what I am, is wholly distinct from the body."[18] For Descartes, the "I" is a rational, cogent agent that has the capability of overcoming the body's fallibility. This basic premise of Cartesian philosophy shaped almost all subsequent approaches to cognitive science and philosophy until recently.

One of Heidegger's most important contributions to philosophy is his attack on Cartesian thinking. For Heidegger, knowledge and understanding come from our interactions with things and with each other, rather than the detached, theoretical formulations of a divorced mind. There is more to the concept of the self than the rational executive function of the mind. There is a bodily component of our interactions with the world:

> Heidegger's important insight is not that, when we solve problems, we sometimes make use of representational equipment outside our bodies, but that being-in-the-world is more basic than thinking and solving problems; that it is not representational at all. That is, when we are coping at our best, we are drawn in by solicitations and respond directly to them, so that the distinction between us and our equipment—between inner and outer—vanishes.[19]

Within this act of coping, the dualisms that Descartes posited are no longer relevant. "Self and world belong together in a single entity, Dasein. Self and world are not two entities, like subject and object...but self and world are the basic determination of Dasein itself in the unity of the structure of being-in-the-world."[20] Given Dasein's situated nature, the differences between subject and object, self and world, become less pronounced, as Being embedded in the world by definition rejects these differences. This allows us to think about certain aspects of the environment as an extension of the mind—things as extensions of bodies—and lays the theoretical groundwork for what we now know as embodied cognition (and its offshoots).

Consider the example of to-do list mobile applications—apps that take the analogue behavior of paper to-do lists and digitize it, layering features that assist with information recall and reminders. These apps speak to many aspects of the modern condition: hyper-productivity, having too much to do, measuring productivity by crossing things off a list, the need to make tangible the things we want to accomplish, etc. But perhaps most importantly, they illustrate our ability to offload memory outside the head. Memory is no longer purely cognitive. Rather, these types of apps acknowledge that our default memory is not adequate and we must use an "external" apparatus to augment it. This, of course, begs the question of whether this apparatus is truly external. Or, can we think of the attainment of goals as something that transcends internal and external categories? Are to-do list apps an augmentation of our internal memory, or do the categories of internal and external no longer apply in this situation, as reliance on the app is often greater than our own "wetware" memory? Technological devices have always been the means by which Dasein interacts with the environment. We're now at a point where these highly personal technological devices—mobile phones, tablets, medical equipment, online banking services, digitized health tracking, etc.—are incorporated even more intimately into the everyday existence of the user.

Cartesian dualism is everywhere in design. We see radical distinctions in the design process between problems and solutions, strategy and tactics, designers and users, theory and practice, thinking and doing. Some of these distinctions exist for good reason, while others create confusion and problems for designers. For example, the designer/user distinction is mostly a product of the movement from craft-based societies where this distinction did not exist, to post Industrial Revolution societies where products needed to not only serve a function, but also communicate meaning to large groups of people—i.e., design projects grew beyond making a pot or a sword. Division of labor and an awareness of end goals pushed these groups apart. On the other hand, the theory/practice and thinking/doing separation is a direct result of Cartesian thinking. In other words, it assumes that there is a theoretical-thinking component of the design process that must occur before the practical-doing functions. While it is easy to sell this process to clients—as it makes sense on a certain gut level—it is far from how design processes actually work. In reality, the entire design team is involved in theoretical, practical, thinking, doing, problem-finding, and solution-articulating activities throughout the process, without much real distinction between "phases." We will return to these concerns in chapter 4 with a discussion of the paradoxes in the design process.

Praxis and Situated Action

Heidegger goes beyond linking self and world through Dasein when he calls for a complete rejection of Cartesian thinking. Instead of an authoritative subject performing mental functions and then acting upon the world, Heidegger asserts that our everyday engaged action with the environment is what brings knowledge and understanding. That is, we formulate what we know about the world by interacting with objects. This does not, however, simply mean that practice precedes theory; there is still an important place for theoretical formulations. Heidegger's point, rather, is that pure theory has less influence on how we interpret the world compared to practical action. That is, thinking about going to a concert and even mentally playing out all the steps involved is radically different from actually going. The former event is divorced from the use context, whereas the latter event provides practical knowledge of the experience. Strict interpretation suggests that understanding cannot happen in the Cartesian mode.

The same works for knowledge of objects: "The functionality that goes with a chair, blackboard, window is exactly that which makes a thing what it is."[21] For Heidegger, the essential qualities of an object are not its physical properties but rather the actions it allows users to perform. We know something by what we do with it. Form essentially means nothing to Heidegger. We could eat cereal with a baseball bat, and that would give it meaning as a cereal-eating device (though likely not a very good one). A phenomenological understanding of interaction notes a difference between acting on and acting through. In one case, the focus is the technology. In another, the focus is the user's end goal. Acting upon an object takes the object itself as the focal point of the interaction, whereas acting through it takes the user's end goal as the focal point. We can apply this type of thinking to almost any given object, from everyday items like spoons and eyeglasses, to more extreme examples such as military drones and city transit systems.

Another distinction between a phenomenological understanding of objects as opposed to a Cartesian understanding is the difference between knowing-that and knowing-how. Hubert Dreyfus, a Heideggerian philosopher who dealt mostly with artificial intelligence systems, explains the difference by evoking the hammer, a common example in early phenomenological discourse: "To understand a hammer, for example, does not mean to know *that* hammers have such and such properties and *that* they are used for certain purposes—or that in order to hammer one follows a certain procedure, i.e., understanding a hammer at its most primordial means *knowing how* to hammer."[22] For Dreyfus, there is a separation between knowing the components of a hammer—that it has a handle one grasps, a hard metal head, one side used to drive a nail, and the other used to remove a nail, etc.—and knowing the physical act of using a hammer to accomplish a goal. That is, practical understanding comes from the latter: by picking up a hammer and using it. Another example is swimming. If a child does not yet know how to swim, parents do not provide him/her with a book on fluid dynamics and expect the child to learn. Instead, the parents take the child swimming to show by example and performance.

Think of the last time you were in a corporate brainstorming session. A group of people gets in a room, most of them present for the free lunch. Someone acting as the facilitator says something like, "just throw out ideas, nothing is too outlandish." A couple alphas start free-associating. One person reacts positively to an idea and everyone else jumps on the bandwagon, so as not to cause any tension. At the end of an hour or so, someone with a fancy title and equally large paycheck makes a decision on what will be built. The process ends there. The problems with this approach include: 1) It assumes everyone in the room has the same base level knowledge of the problem space, and 2) the outputs are simply theoretical assumptions based on current knowledge, not practical knowledge, of the deeper situation. Contrast this approach with design methodologies dealing with rapid prototyping. A team might begin with a similar brainstorming exercise, but there is an understanding that the end results are not necessarily design directions. They are assumptions to be tested with real users in the real world. A good design team will prototype multiple solutions to take into the world to test. This approach takes the theory developed in the first session, and then extends it into the spaces where it really matters, creating a layer of praxical knowledge.

Thus far, experience designers have maintained a separation between practice and theory. We often see theory as more of the "intellectual," speculative side, and practice as the executional side. Although Heidegger quite explicitly prioritizes practice over theory in his attack on Cartesian philosophy, he leaves the door open for the idea of praxis. In its most basic form, praxis is theoretically-informed practice. It allows us to think about practice beyond the empty pantomime that can be such an unfortunate, but integral, part of much design practice. Praxical knowledge is that which is embodied in everyday experience, but is also informed by theoretical reflection. In a certain sense, praxis takes the rigor of theory and embeds it into practical action. We can also interpret praxis in the Aristotelian sense[23] as a process in which the emphasis is on the process itself, as opposed to the final product. That is, praxis is about action over making; it allows for the emergence of new ideas through process, rather than executing on a pre-set plan. The most obvious example from experience design is sketching. We sketch not to create client-ready documents but rather to help us think. Sketching is literally externalized thought, which we can throw out, revise, or use as a point of discussion.

Praxis is (or at least it should be) the domain of design professionals, not only because it provides rigor to design methods, but also because it forces the recognition of use contexts: "[T]ools are not simply objects that have certain qualities. Rather, what a tool is, is dependent on a *use context*. [...] [T]he kind of 'knowledge' that arises in praxis is *not* cognitive, Cartesian-type knowledge; it is, rather, a use knowledge in which the tool or equipment becomes a *means* of accomplishment."[24] The situational context of an object provides its thing-ly qualities. A baseball bat lying on the ground is a meaningless object. But when picked up and used, it becomes a tool to play sports or an instrument of violence (or a tool to eat cereal), depending on the context. Praxis allows us to explore these use contexts by removing, or decreasing, the compulsive need for immediate finality. Prototypes and unfinished things let designers play, focus on processes of action, and account for the inherent variability of design. This variability of use contexts is something that post-phenomenological thinkers have focused on as a bit of a wrench in the design machine. We'll deal with that in later chapters.

Interaction Patterns

Heidegger's *Being and Time* is a long, laborious text that becomes more demanding the more one interacts with it. Core to his thinking about objects is his famous "tool analysis," through which he examines the ways in which we interact with objects, or "equipment." His analysis centers on two poles of interaction: *Vorhandenheit* and *Zuhandenheit*, commonly and awkwardly translated into English as present-at-hand and ready-to-hand.

Presence-at-hand is a relationship with an object defined by theoretical knowledge and scientific observation. In this mode, the object is observed as wholly separate from the observer. It is factual and analyzable from afar. The present-at-hand relationship is one of decontextualization and detached speculation. Returning to the example of the baseball bat: when the bat is laying on the ground and not in use, the observer assumes a present-at-hand relationship and examines the functional components of the object but not its contexts of use.

Readiness-to-hand is a human-object relationship based on active engagement. In this mode, the object is a tool for accomplishing a certain goal, becoming an extension of the user's body. The user *acts through* the object to attain a goal, as opposed to acting *with* or *upon* the object, providing a sense of fluidity in the engagement. The object itself fades into the background of interaction, and becomes part of the background relations that shape behavior but are outside the direct consciousness of the user. Readiness-to-hand is the essence of Heidegger's observation that Dasein always exists ahead of itself—through constant attainment of goals, we exist as Dasein oriented to that future event.

While these two categories of interaction are different, we should not necessarily view them as separate and distinct categories. In many cases, we can think of them on a continuum. Consider the example of typing an email. If you are fluent with a standard keyboard, your focus while typing is likely not on the keys but rather on your message, how the reader might interpret your message, and what words you should choose. Your relationship to the keyboard is one of readiness-to-hand: you are *acting through* the keyboard *in order to* accomplish the goal of sending the email. The keyboard itself fades into the background of the experience. Now imagine if, while typing, you misspell a word. At that moment, your ready-to-hand relationship with the keyboard is broken, since you now need to go back and consciously re-type the word. The keyboard has become present-at-hand as an object of concern and deliberation.

Paul Dourish provides a particularly lucid and relevant example:

> These are ways, Heidegger explains, that we encounter the world and act through it. As an example, consider the mouse connected to my computer. Much of the time, I act through the mouse; the mouse is an extension of my hand as I select objects, operate menus, and so forth. The mouse is, in Heidegger's terms, ready-to-hand. Sometimes, however, such as when I reach the edge of the mouse pad and cannot move the mouse further, my orientation toward the mouse changes. Now, I become conscious of the mouse mediating my action, precisely because of the fact that it has been interrupted. The mouse becomes the object of my attention as I pick it up and move it back to the center of the mouse pad. When I act on the mouse in this way, being mindful of

it as an object of my activity, the mouse is present-at-hand. Heidegger does more than point out that we have different ways of orienting toward objects; his observation is more radical. He argues that the mouse exists for us as an entity only because of the way in which it can become present-at-hand, and becomes equipment only through the way in which it can be ready-to-hand. And in being ready-to-hand, it disappears from view—or 'withdraws'—as an independent entity: The ready-to-hand is not grasped theoretically at all.... The peculiarity of what is proximally ready-to-hand is that, in its readiness-to-hand, it must, as it were, withdraw in order to be ready-to-hand quite authentically. That with which our everyday dealings proximally dwell is not the tools themselves. On the contrary, that with which we concern ourselves primarily is the work. In other words, as we act through technology that has become ready-to-hand, the technology itself disappears from our immediate concerns. We are caught up in the performance of the work; our mode of being is one of 'absorbed coping.' The equipment fades into the background.[25]

There are a few things to note about this passage:

1) The ready-to-hand relationship is characterized by withdrawal.

In Dourish's example, the computer mouse disappears from the interaction as the user acts through it to accomplish small, discrete goals related to larger goals. This disappearance is quite literal. In the ready-to-hand relationship, the user orients him/herself to a future goal, and the object becomes a transparent means to accomplishment. For Heidegger, this is what defines "equipmentality": the nature of equipment is its transparency with regard to user intention.

2) Interruptions cause a shift in interaction style.

The breaking of smooth interaction—in this case defined by reaching the edge of the mouse pad—shifts the relationship to one of presence-at-hand. The user must consciously and deliberately consider the mouse as an object as they move it back to the middle of the mouse pad. These types of interruptions are inevitable. While much of the design and testing processes aim to minimize the frequency and level of frustration involved with this shift from ready-to-hand to present-at-hand, in the end, the contextual nature of object use will always result in breakage. The important consideration is how users are able to cope with these breaks.

3) Shift in interaction style causes a change in mindfulness, which defines presence-at-hand.
    The movement from ready-to-hand to present-at-hand is a shift in mindfulness and attention. In the former, the user is not conscious of the object as such. While in the latter, the object is recognized as an object to be acted upon.

    The vast majority of our dealings with the world are within the ready-to-hand mode. In this sense, phenomenology is a very mundane philosophy, as it is concerned with not only the highly significant and influential phenomena, but also with the day-to-day experiences that shape the background of existence. It is concerned with how we experience the chair on which we are currently sitting and, perhaps more importantly, the shift in consciousness from before you read the previous sentence to after. It is likely you were not conscious of the chair (if you are currently using one), and it was operating as a ready-to-hand means of sitting. Now that you are conscious of it as an object, the relationship has switched to the present-at-hand, and you reflect on the chair as an object. This concern with the everyday experience is particularly important for experience design, as humans spend their waking moments interacting with things. There is a constant movement between the present-at-hand and ready-to-hand in everyday life, and designing with that movement in mind is the job of experience designers.

Reflecting on the Object Experience
    Now that we have laid some groundwork on the basics of Heideggerian phenomenology, it is useful to reflect on the concepts presented thus far within the context of object use. We have seen that Dasein is oriented toward the future as a situated being within the world, the implications being that Dasein constantly reaches out to its environment for areas of focus, incorporates objects into itself, and extends beyond the body while still maintaining the body as the primary mode of action. Dasein uses objects to know the world, and thus objects stand in a strange place within the self-world relationship: they are "in-between" self and world, but are also an inherent part of the self-world system.

We turn again to Samuel Beckett's novel *Malone Dies* to illustrate some key components of the Dasein-object relationship. Malone spends a lot of time reflecting on his things. His opinions range from love to hatred, in a wonderful example of Beckett's ability to convey ambivalence.

> I have rummaged a little in my things, sorting them out and drawing them over to me, to look at them. I was not far wrong in thinking that I knew them off, by heart, and could speak of them at any moment, without looking at them. But I wanted to make sure. It was well I did. For now I know that the image of these objects, with which I have lulled myself till now, though accurate in the main, was not completely so. And I should be sorry to let slip this unique occasion which seems to offer me the possibility of something suspiciously like a true statement at last.[26]

Malone's activities while lying on the bed with his objects are suspiciously similar to how users of technological devices interact with screen-based objects. It is no surprise anymore that we use things like mobile phones as physical instantiations of memory: contact lists, calendars, collaborative note-taking, etc. all enable us to offload memory resources to the device and the software that runs it. Much in the same way as we organize our devices, customize them, bring certain information near and move other information farther away, Malone uses his stick to bring objects close to inspect them and push them away when finished. The difference, of course, is that Malone is working in physical space while we are in digital space. The "nearness" and "far-ness" of information for us is not a proximal one but rather a cognitive one. For Heidegger, discussions of near and far were rarely about physical space; they are about the orientation of Dasein.[27] So when we move through mobile phone applications—pushing some to the background to focus on one at hand—we are pushing and pulling, much like Malone. And like Malone, who inspects his objects in order to seek truth, we interact with these devices to discover something, to accomplish a goal, and to reassure ourselves of what we believe to know.

Malone tells us that his stick "has a hook at one end. Thanks to it I can control the furthest recesses of my abode. How great is my debt to sticks! So great that I almost forget the blows they have transferred to me."[28] Despite his focus on objects, it is somewhat rare that Malone specially calls out the *design* of the object itself. In the previous passage, Malone is doing two things: 1) He is telling the reader about how his stick is hooked at one end, so he can use it to grab other objects within range and bring them closer. The stick is literally Malone's only means by which he can manipulate his environment beyond what is within arm's reach on the bed. It has become an extension of his body, much like a wrench to a plumber, brush to a painter, or steering wheel to a driver. 2) He describes his stick as an object of affection and ambivalence. He loves the stick to the point where he can forget about the violence that other sticks have inflicted upon him in the past, but at the same time, he is still aware of that past violence—similar to our love/hate relationship with mobile devices. They are objects of affection—even sharing our beds in some instances—and objects of hate in certain social situations. We love the connectivity they afford but hate the burden of availability.

How can we think of Malone as a metaphor for technology use? He is obviously interacting with basic technologies—sticks, carts, pencils—but his reliance on them, ambivalence to them, and awareness of their design is similar to our current situation. One of the most profound effects of mobile computing hitting the mainstream, I think, is not necessarily the technology itself, but the relationships we have begun to form with our devices. It sounds a bit cliché, but I believe general statements around our reliance on mobile technology are true. We become anxious without our phones, as they are the material substantiation of so much social activity. Mobile devices are like clusters of affordances that allow a massive amount of work and social activity to be completed easily and efficiently. But at the same time, we are ambivalent toward phones. We scoff when someone takes a call in an inappropriate setting; we get annoyed if our dinner date checks his/her phone too many times; and we are quickly reaching a point at which the information provided by our phones is simply too much. In a very real sense, our phones are not phones anymore—they are more like pocket computers. This sense of providing too much information makes us hyper-aware of design, and (for digital technology in general) has created entire new industries aimed at improving the ease of use for products we interact with everyday.

Usability, for example, is the process by which designers determine the effectiveness of their designs. It aims to study the ease of use for a particular object—whether labels are clear, functionality is according to expectation, users can complete necessary tasks, etc. These tasks and the means by which we measure ease of use are usually quite mechanical. Can users determine how to complete the purchase process? Can users effectively sign up for an account? Still, there is also a less pragmatic side to usability that deals with things like whether the product is effectively communicating a design intention, or whether it meets overall expectations based on competitive products. Additionally, there is the sense that user testing and usability can result in a social learning process.[29] That is, through testing a prototype, the designer is facilitating an educational goal. Tonkinwise's example in the above-cited video is Apple's iPad. By releasing products in generations, Apple was able to teach the public about portable music files (iPod), the pocket computer we like to call a "phone" (iPhone), and eventually the iPad. What this evolution did was educate the public about the potentiality of computing outside the home precisely so that Apple could introduce cloud to the in-home experience with the iPad. By taking smaller steps, they were able to introduce revolutionary products without rupturing the entire system, not to mention sell more products in different incarnations.

While we might not ever escape the effects of information abundance, we have, however, developed ways to cope with it. Our relationship to modern technology is one of ambivalence, but as humans, we are quite good at coping with the world.

> Hubert Dreyfus was the first to articulate an account of practical coping which he defines as the 'mostly smooth and unobtrusive responsiveness to circumstances that enable human beings to get around in the world.' Dreyfus proposes practical coping as an alternative to classical accounts of cognition, which involve the application of "rules" to an internal representation as a means to create plans which are duly executed. Thus coping is the practical, skillful and representation-free dealing with the world and, of course, technology.[30]

Coping works on a few levels. Colloquially, we think of coping as dealing with something that is broken or inadequate in some way, or dealing with a non-optimal situation. We might cope with the death of a loved one by grieving, or cope with a wobbly table by placing a folded piece of paper under one of the legs. But coping, according to Dreyfus, occurs on a more mundane level than the type of conscious coping just described. We cope with the world simply by interacting with things. The ready-to-hand relationship is a smooth coping, whereas the present-at-hand might be thought of as a rupture of smooth coping that results in conscious awareness. We can also think of coping as an everyday design process, as a way to actively manage the environment.

In this sense, user testing is a means of determining coping strategies. Too often we think of testing as a mechanical process by which we eliminate the problematic aspects of a product. This view is the type of worldview that Dreyfus was trying to debunk in his work on artificial intelligence. While at MIT, Dreyfus observed that early AI programmers were taking a rule-based Cartesian view of the human mind, and attempting to replicate it within a computer. That is, if we can reduce the world to a set of facts and program a computer to know all of those facts, we would eventually land on a piece of software that understands the world as a human. Of course, this goal has yet to become a reality. Dreyfus would argue that the AI project failed because humans don't actually perceive the world as a set of facts but rather as a system contextual interactions and potentialities. We cope with the environment based on what it makes possible for us.

This implies that things do not have properties in themselves but only in relation to their context of use: "When the hammer I am using fails to work and I cannot immediately get another, I have to deal with it as too heavy, unbalanced, broken, etc. These characteristics belong to the hammer only as used by me in a specific situation. *Being too heavy* is certainly not a *property* of the hammer."[31] In a user testing situation, our interest is not necessarily what properties the product has—it is how users are able to cope with it. We gather knowledge about the background relations the object affords, whether it assists in meaning creation, and coping strategies. Observing coping strategies and building that insight back into the design process is a more genuine way of testing, as opposed to the more positivist approach of determining and eliminating the 'unintuitive' aspects of a product.

The unfortunate tendency for designers working with commercial clients is to eliminate, or at least provide the illusion that they have eliminated, the undesirable aspects of a product. They fear instability and complexity. My point is not to claim that usability is unimportant—it is to illustrate how breakage is unavoidable:

> Breakdowns are a necessary accompaniment to design, not because the designer lacks competence, but because of the nature of the design process. A breakdown is not a negative situation which one has to avoid. It is the situation of what is not self-

evident. A breakdown reveals the tissue of the relations needed to fulfill the tasks. From this follows a clear target for design: anticipating the forms of breakdowns and opening up possibilities for the action in case they happen.[32]

There is a positive effect of breakdowns that only reveals itself in the moment of interaction. So even when a product breaks within the testing process, Bonsiepe points out in the passage above that it "reveals the tissue of the relations needed to fulfill tasks." The act of breaking shows designers something that was not anticipated. The next step, then, is not necessarily (or at least not *only*) to eradicate the cause of the breakdown, but to learn how it affects the entire system of interaction. The anxiety felt from breakdowns causes designers to focus their efforts on pure eradication, either because of client pressure or their own need for perfection.

The fear of an imperfectly functioning product is summed up in a particularly interesting word that often comes up in consumer-facing design: abandonment. The fickle nature of interactions with mobile phones especially has created an environment of anxiety around product adoption and cessation. We are told that unusable products are abandoned because if people cannot immediately (or 'intuitively') use them, they will not put in the time to learn them. I was recently talking with a friend and colleague about the iPad app for Spotify, a music service. She was trying to get her songs to shuffle but could not find the correct button. Eventually, we discovered the button buried in a screen that had little to do with actually playing the music; it was not part of the main controls. This interaction and subsequent frustration sparked a conversation about the importance of usability compared to the perceived value a product brings. Since all of her music is on Spotify, she is willing to cope with design details that frustrate her as opposed to "abandoning" it. Another example is Seamless, a food ordering service. Their website and mobile applications are filled with poor taxonomy, dead ends, and ambiguous error messages, breaking the most basic of usability heuristics. The service, however, continues to be popular, especially among urban dwellers who have little time and space to cook frequently. There is something about the utility Seamless and Spotify provide that trumps their less-than-ideal design details.

Not only do these points of breakage rupture smooth coping, but they also make the product (or object) "conspicuous":

When equipment malfunctions, Heidegger says, we discover its unsuitability by the 'circumspection of the dealings in which we use it,' and the equipment thereby becomes 'conspicuous.' '*Conspicuousness* presents the available equipment in a certain unassailableness.' But for most normal ways of coping, so that after a moment of being startled, and seeing a meaningless object, we shift to a new way of coping and go on.[33]

The smooth coping experience is marked by deep involvement. The user in the ready-to-hand mode is in a state of action without conscious thought. Common examples of users in such states are jazz musicians, carpenters, and other craft-based professionals. Given the improvisational aspects of jazz, jazz musicians are known to become particularly wrapped up in their craft. They do not simply play an instrument—they pay attention to the other musicians on stage, audience reactions, environmental cues, etc. to create a holistic system of music. Some describe becoming "one with their instrument," or in other words, their instrument becomes an extension of their body to the point where only a major rupture will interrupt the interaction. Since they are within the improvisational system, small interruptions such as playing the wrong note are not terribly detrimental. It would take something like a breakdown in rhythm to interrupt the flow and make the entire band's instruments conspicuous. If the drummer is off in his or her timing, the entire band must adjust their rhythm after their instruments become "disembodied" as present-at-hand objects. The instruments shift from embodied to conspicuous.

A similar thing happens in everyday object use. Returning to the previous example of Spotify, we come up with ways to cope with the object because it provides a certain amount of value. So the cause for actual product abandonment is not simply "bad usability"—it is "bad usability" relative to the value and meaning the product provides. Users abandon things not when usability is less than desirable, but when they become meaningless:

> Because meanings always extend beyond actual senses, they may lead to unfulfilled expectations. A computer freezes unexpectedly. A wrong turn is taken at an intersection. We cut our finger. A usually reliable tool breaks unexpectedly. Martin Heidegger (Dreyfus, 1992:77ff.) calls such a condition "breakdown." However, what breaks down is neither the artifact (although it is

indeed possible that it falls apart unpredictably) nor the users' concepts or memories (although they too could be inappropriate, drift, and lose touch with "reality"). What breaks down is the meaningfulness of the interface of which we are a part. This happens when meanings and actions lead us to expect something that is contradicted by what is sensed, when expected and actual senses deviate significantly.[34]

Usability, then, is not necessarily a functionalist mode of determining user-friendliness, or at least this mode is insufficient. Meaning provides a facet of usability that forces designers to think past function into the domains of culture, language, and everyday practice. "User-friendliness is not merely an issue of the number of errors made per unit of time. It is rooted in the confidence of being able to handle disruptions. Design can support that confidence."[35] Similar to Tonkinwise's thoughts on the social learning aspects of user testing, the design process can aid users in facilitating understanding of a product, as opposed to simple knowledge. When users have knowledge of product function, their expectations of how it will function are often inflated. As we will see later, the use and function of objects are different. By facilitating understanding, designers open up possibilities of use beyond pre-determined use cases, and thus a user can see beyond a particular use case into an entire world of potential actions. This freedom allows for coping with interruptions in ways that might not be possible when the approach to usability is simply function-based.

A final point on functionalist usability is made so eloquently by Klaus Krippendorff:

> Taylorism is an effort to organize the workplace for the sake of efficiency. Cost–benefit analysis feeds into efficiency concerns by using money as the unit of measurement. In gauging usability, error rates, the number of steps needed to reach an objective, the time taken to learn an interface, all measure the lack of efficiency. The whole idea of optimizing, maximizing, or satisficing a scarce resource has a long tradition in northern European culture, in which it is equated with (technological) rationality, with uniform standards applicable everywhere and to everybody. The industrial era was dominated by criteria that served the industry more so than users.[36]

It is ironic that the movement we know as user-centered design was in some sense a reaction against Taylorist management—which attempted to quantify and optimize a workforce—when, at the same time, the activities involved with usability are often quite mechanistic. User-centered design claims to treat users as individuals, and this means it must embrace the messiness of being human along with our ability to cope, find meaning, and adapt to challenges.

Heidegger on Technology

In *Being and Time*, Heidegger traces out the ways that humans sought to gain knowledge of the world, going back to the ancient Greeks and Romans. Plato and Aristotle relied on the concept of *physis* (the natural form or shape of something) to explain the relationship between art and the natural world. As opposed to *techne* (to make something appear, usually through art, craft, and the work of the hands), *physis* is a nature that arises out of itself. If *techne* requires human intervention—that is, one who shapes—*physis* is form without intervention.

Related to *physis* is *poiesis*, or what Heidegger calls bringing-forth. In its most obvious modern equivalent, the poetical mode is one in which meaning emerges out of a pre-existing state. The poet does not necessarily impose meaning onto the world; s/he finds points in the world that are meaningful and extracts them out into their full potential. The arts are a very pure poetical form in that they interpret the world in unique ways that reveals a sense of truth. Art is a hermeneutics of the world—one which is constantly reinterpreted through its provocations. *Techne* is commonly translated as art, craft, or skill, but Heidegger points out that the essence of its meaning lies in the intentional act of making something appear. It is the practical side of *poiesis* in the sense that it encapsulates the idea that human intervention is a necessary part of the process.

Heidegger worked to articulate the relationship between these three forms of knowing the world (among a few others) in terms of where they overlap and where they are opposed. The result is his theory of technological understanding of the world. For Heidegger, the next evolution of understanding is through technology. As we will see, Heidegger was far from a techno-optimist; he was quite skeptical about dependence on technology and its ability to force humans into a passive position. The following will attempt to summarize and critique Heidegger's work on technology, stemming mostly from his essay *The Question*

Concerning Technology. We will return to many of the critical remarks in later chapters on post-phenomenology.

Much of Heidegger's thinking on technology revolves around the following statement: "All that is merely technological never arrives at the essence of technology."[37] I must admit, as esoteric and vague as his writing can be (especially in translation), this sentence has been a particular source of confusion for some time. What Heidegger seems to be saying is that there is something more to technology that individual pieces of technology can never contain. This sentiment stems from his critique of instrumentalism, or the view that technology is simply a means to an end. "Technology is not equivalent to the essence of technology. When we are seeking the essence of 'tree,' we have to become aware that that which pervades every tree, as tree, is not itself a tree that can be encountered among all other trees. Likewise, the essence of technology is by no means anything technological."[38] This is so confusing because it seems to contradict much of Heidegger's earlier thinking on the nature of Dasein, self and world, and the critique of Cartesianism. What he suggests is a sort of transcendental, pseudo-Platonic ideal of technology that fails to express itself fully through technological objects. There is something about technology that exists at a higher level than individual objects can access. Given Heidegger's focus on our interactions with objects in his early work, it is surprising that this later essay shifts to a more Platonic vision of technology.

The notion of a separate, decontextualized idea of technology would have been absurd to the early Heidegger. But in his essay on technology, we find Heidegger coming very close to contradicting his earlier thought on the expression of equipment through the ready-to-hand mode. Many Heidegger scholars call this switch in view—among some other differences between early and late work—The Turn. Heidegger himself even recognized the turn in his thinking, but this topic remains a mysterious one.

> Indeed, Heidegger argues that it is just this nontechnological 'essence' that has been obscured by the commonly accepted definition of technology as instrumental, as a means to an end. For Heidegger, this instrumental conception of technology—although it presumes to define 'what technology is;' to define 'the technological'—is merely the modern manifestation of 'the essence of technology.' In other words, the modern conception of

technology, because it restricts the definition of the technological to instrumental terms, 'blinds us to' that broader 'essence' that informs not only the modern view of technology, but also the quite different conceptions of traditional technology and the techne of ancient Greece.[39]

Heidegger was a techno-pessimist, or at least a modern-techno-pessimist. By this time in his career, he began to move away from thinking about objects through the ready-to-hand mode as instruments of accomplishment, and toward the non-instrumental vision of technology we see here. His examination of modern technology is full of nostalgia and romantic notions of ancient Greek conceptions of technology. Heidegger believed that modern technology conceived as a means to an end does not do justice to the Greek versions of *techne* and *poeisis*, or "making" and "bringing-forth."

> For Heidegger, this 'essence of technology' cannot simply be defined in terms of the usual, modern sense of technology as an instrument, tool, or machine. He attempts instead to broaden the notion of technology into a more general concept of making or producing, including artistic production. The 'essence of technology' is therefore not a static conceptual category or ideal, but a dynamic, ongoing process or movement.[40]

We get the sense from Rutsky that Heidegger was simply linking technology to a type of production in the same category as art and craft. While partially true, I think the real value concerns the potential for technology to reveal something that was not visible before. It helps bring the background to the foreground, and vice versa. Technology, then, is similar to art in its ability to "read" the world.

Heidegger's essay on technology revolves around a few key themes that deserve to be examined closer: bringing-forth and challenging-forth, standing reserve, and enframing. Heidegger articulates *techne* as that which reveals: "Techne [...] reveals whatever does not bring itself forth and does not yet lie here before us, whatever can look and turn out now one way and now another."[41] The act of making is not simply the creation of an object but also a practice in revealing a sense of truth about the world. There is something beyond the object-ness of the object. This is the hermeneutic quality of technology. Affecting that which is beyond the object is a primary concern for experience design. This is essentially the "experience," from the meaning a user associates with a designed object to the role it plays in their everyday life. In a sense, the designer takes that which is "concealed," then recognizes its qualities and extracts meaning in the form of an object.

It is worth noting that the German phrase Heidegger uses to describe this bringing-forth is *das Entbergen*. Broken into its parts, *ent* means "forth," "out," or the sense of negating a previous condition. *Bergen* is to rescue or keep safe through concealment. So *das Entbergen* is literally "bringing-forth what was safely hidden." Here we see the common trope within Heidegger's work that Graham Harman[42] identified: the opposition between concealment and unconcealment, the veiled and the unveiled. What is perhaps more interesting is the sense of safety. If *das Entbergen* is to reveal what was safely hidden, the obvious question is why there was a need to hide in the first place. What is the threat?

There is a shift in *The Question Concerning Technology* from bringing-forth to challenging-forth once Heidegger begins to talk more specifically about *modern* technology.

> What is modern technology? It too is a revealing. Only when we allow our attention to rest on this fundamental characteristic does that which is new in modern technology show itself to us. And yet the revealing that holds sway throughout modern technology does not unfold into a bringing-forth in the sense of *poeisis*. That revealing that rules in modern technology is a challenging, which puts to nature the unreasonable demand that it supply energy that can be extracted and stored as such.[43]

Again, a note on the original German is helpful. *Herausfordern* is the German word used, which literally translates to "challenge," but can also be used to indicate provocation or defiance. We get the sense that modern technology is somehow special because it defies *poeisis* and institutes a new form of revelation based on the ability to extract and store energy. As we will see, Heidegger is not terribly specific about what this "energy" is. Nonetheless, there is a strange sort of nostalgic romanticism in this passage. Heidegger is lamenting the loss of *poeisis* as modern technology defies nature all around him.

[Heidegger] illustrates his theory with the contrast between a silver chalice made by a Greek craftsman and a modern dam on the Rhine. The craftsman gathers the elements—form, matter, finality—and thereby brings out the 'truth' of his materials. Modern technology 'de-worlds' its materials and 'summons' (*Herausfordern*) nature to submit to extrinsic demands. Instead of a world of authentic beings capable of gathering a rich variety of contexts and meanings, we are left with an 'objectless' heap of functions.[44]

Another distinction we might make between *techne*, or craft-based activities (such as the creation of a chalice), and design (such as the river dam) is that *techne* exists for the craftsperson while design exists for others. We will have much more to say about design and craft in the next chapter. For now, it is sufficient to conclude that the craftsperson creates for him/herself, gathering materials and crafting an object based on personal objectives, or at least for a relatively small number of people. The designer, on the other hand, works with modern technology—s/he creates for others, and subsequently, according to Heidegger, strips materials of their worldliness.

This is the threat from which the world hides. As modern technology manifests itself—i.e., is designed—nature is challenged to reveal itself in ways that Heidegger deems "unreasonable."

The standing reserve—sometimes translated as "resource well" or "stock"—is a very familiar concept to contemporary experience designers. Practitioner's publications are filled with articles espousing the "invisibility" of technology, and how we should be striving toward creating "intuitive" interfaces. What this discourse points to is the sense that we can design technology in such a way that it is "here when needed and gone when not." This is the promise of Mark Wieser's "calm computing"[45] that has yet to be fully realized, but is certainly evolving quickly.

The standing reserve is a sort of pool of technological energy we can tap into at any time. It is a hoard of *stuff* that stands by in wait: "Everywhere everything is ordered to stand by, to be immediately at hand, indeed to stand there just so that it may be on called for a further ordering. Whatever is ordered about in this way has its own standing. We call it the standing-reserve [*Bestand*]. [...] Whatever stands by in the sense of standing-reserve no longer stands over against us as object."[46] By welling up nature into a standing reserve, Heidegger argues that we block out *poeisis* in favor of a more artificial revealing via technology. The most obvious contemporary example is the smartphone. These devices are essentially bundles of affordances that allow an almost infinite number of actions and access to an almost infinite amount of information, nestled conveniently in our pocket waiting to be called upon. The mobile device literally waits in our pants pocket, waiting to be called upon. Heidegger's fear is that the standing reserve places the user is a passive position to technology.

More specifically, the past decade has seen advances in the field of context-aware computing as a form of ubiquitous computing that senses and adapts to a user's context, usually measured via location, movement, and time. Depending on these variables, context-aware applications are able to serve information particularly relevant to the user's context, and remain inert when the context calls for a lack of distraction. Popular examples include many in-car systems that will switch a phone to voice recognition and feedback when it detects movement, so the user can concentrate on the road. Another is Google Now: a context-aware system Google has built directly into their operating system. It is able to make connections between calendar items, location, weather data, traffic conditions, recently visited websites, etc. to serve information—alerts for when to leave for an upcoming appointment according to traffic or public transit; notifications on when a package has been shipped and tracking information; suggestions on things to do based on current location; etc.

The topic of "invisible" interfaces is essentially a fantasy that involves creating an interface so "intuitive" that it does not need to be called upon, as it only reveals itself at the exact time a user needs it. While this project's motives and potential for success are dubious, it nonetheless shows how the standing reserve functions within contemporary experience design. The fantasy of zero user involvement begins to trump questions of whether interfaces *should* be invisible in the first place. We will critique these points in later chapters.

A final example that deserves mention here is productivity and to-do list management applications. The motive behind these products largely revolves around productivity and optimization. By managing an intelligent to-do list, one not only outsources memory but also calls upon that stock of memory in order to feel productive. The focus becomes more about *feeling* productive rather than actually *being* productive, as the user offloads the ethical matter of task completion onto the piece of technology. One shores up that digital feeling of accomplishment until it's time to cash in.

Heidegger applied his thinking on the standing reserve to all modern technology, and the examples here are simply some extreme contemporary instantiations. Certainly, if we follow Heidegger's lead, we can continue the list of examples *ad infinitum*. The pervasiveness of the standing reserve influences Heidegger to classify our relationship with modern technology as an enframing, or the gathering of technologically stored energy as it reveals itself to us. The onus is on experience designers to responsibly design these systems, and preserve the relationship between user and system.

Making Sense of Technology

At its core, phenomenology is concerned with how we make sense of the world, and the objects we use are the means by which the world reveals itself. The objects we take for granted and use every day—spoons, keyboards, doorknobs, mobile devices, books, cars, etc.—all have unique ways of revealing the world to users. Both phenomenologists and designers are keenly aware and concerned with this idea, as design, like art and technology, is a hermeneutic activity. We use design to interpret the world.

Whereas most of Heidegger's work focused on this lofty ideal of *poeisis* and how technology reveals truth, contemporary philosophy of technology tends to narrow its concentration down to everyday things. Everyday objects are the means through which we understand the world, though their significance is often veiled by their everyday-ness. That is, their ubiquity leads results in a perceived lack of importance. Contemporary phenomenology and philosophy of technology and design are now attempting to bring these objects back into focus. In a certain sense, contemporary philosophy of technology and design are taking a sort of default phenomenological stance.

I will do my best to substantiate that claim throughout the remainder of this book, beginning with an examination of the relationship between things and meaning. Our ability to experience a thing is dependent on our ability to make sense of the object. Knowledge is an integral part of interactions with things. Dasein is in a constant state of making sense of its surroundings—as an active process of contextual engagement, Dasein is always reaching out to the environment and using objects to make sense of how it relates to the world. But how does one "make sense?" Klaus Krippendorff reminds us that "making sense always entails a bit of a paradox between the aim of making something new and different from what was there before, and the desire to have it make sense, to be recognizable and understandable. The former calls for innovation, while the latter calls for the reproduction of historical continuities."[47] So the question is whether Dasein interacts with the world and extracts meaning, or the interaction itself creates meaning. Traditional phenomenology might say that meaning exists in the world, and our active engagement is a means of interpretation. The ambiguity of "making sense," however, urges us to also consider that interpretation is a more involved activity than simply the decoding of meaning.

We have previously covered the intimate connection between individuals and their context. Individuals literally have no existence divorced from the network of relations that makes up the context phenomenon, and similarly, objects have no meaning outside their context of use. In his examination of product semantics, Krippendorff creates a direct link between meaning and an individual's ability to imagine user contexts: "What some thing is (the totality of what it means) to someone corresponds to the sum total of its imaginable contexts. A knife has all kinds of uses; cutting is merely the most prominent one. Prying open a box, tightening a screw, scraping paint from a surface, cleaning dirty fingernails are as imaginable as picking a pickle from a pickle jar."[48] Beyond a purely functionalist view of object meaning, Krippendorff suggests that meaning accounts for all possible use contexts, and not simply the most common one. We will return to this idea in chapter 5. For now, we turn to a Heideggerian account of things.

Heidegger's concept of Dasein is strangely non-centered—it has no tangible anchoring point we can identify and to which we can say "this is Dasein." Rather, Dasein extends itself out to objects in the world: "[Dasein] finds itself primarily in things because, tending them, distressed by them, it always in some way or other rests in things. Each one of us is what he pursues and cares for. In everyday terms, we understand ourselves and our existence by way of the activities we pursue and the things we take care of."[49] Even if specific devices do no get at the "essence" of technology (as we saw earlier), Heidegger cannot completely discount the importance of individual objects. Dasein is a terribly unstable concept in that without a means with which to manifest and concern itself, it fades away into the background. Dasein's key attribute is, therefore, care—it is concerned with surrounding things and finds its own meaning in them.

In a sort of classic move, Heidegger separates out the things with which we are currently concerned…and everything else:

The *nearest things* that surround us we call *equipment*. There is always already a manifold of equipment: equipment for working, for traveling, for measuring, and in general things with which we have to do. What is given to us primarily is the unity of an *equipmental whole*, a unity that constantly varies in range, expanding or contracting, and that is expressly visible to us for the most part only in excerpts. The *equipmental contexture* of things, for example, the contexture of things as they surround us here, stands in view, but not for the contemplator as though we were sitting here in order to describe the things, not even in the sense of a contemplation that dwells with them.[50]

We should first point out the mention of "nearness." While Heidegger is concerned here with the types of things currently "at-hand" in the form of equipment, he is not necessarily thinking about physical proximity. "Nearness" refers more to the extent to which an object is part of a user's current orientation in the world—e.g., whether the object is in use or not—rather than how close the object is in physical space. For example, your clothing is physically close to your body, but you were likely not concerned with your clothing until you read those words. They were physically near, but praxically far away. The book/tablet you are currently holding, however, is proximally close. Similarly, when Dasein is translated as being-in-the-world, the "in" refers to being concerned with the world rather than being enclosed in some kind of world container.

Heidegger also mentions that the world of equipment exists as an "equipmental whole," but only presents itself to us as "excerpts." That is, there is a foreground and background to the world, and we can only be concerned with a finite amount of information at any given time. This sentiment is not new, but Heidegger gives us the sense that the equipmental context(ure) is experienced rather than analyzed. In that sense, even the act of speaking/writing/reading about equipment frames our point of view as an excerpt of the equipmental whole. This account seems limiting at first, but these excerpts of the whole are what allow us to cope with the world. Otherwise, we would literally be lost in objects. By framing our point of view, we turn objects into things:

> Nearness, it seems, cannot be encountered directly. We succeed in reaching it rather by attending to what is near. Near to us are what we usually call things. But what is a thing? Man has so far given no more thought to the thing as a thing than he has to nearness. The jug is a thing. What is the jug? We say: a vessel, something of the

kind that holds something else within it. The jug's holding is done by its base and sides. This container itself can again be held by the handle. As a vessel the jug is something self-sustained, something that stands on its own. This standing on its own characterizes the jug as something that is self-supporting, or independent. As the self-supporting independence of something independent, the jug differs from an object. An independent, self-supporting thing may become an object if we place it before us, whether in immediate perception or by bringing it to mind in a recollective representation. However, the thingly character of the thing does not consist in its being a represented object, nor can it be defined in any way in terms of objectness, the over-againstness, of the object. The jug remains a vessel whether we represent it in our minds or not.[51]

Nearness becomes not only what is close at hand but also what has meaning for a user here and now. The thing-ness of a thing is determined by our ability to make sense of it. In his example of the jug, Heidegger continues to explain that the thing is something that holds a sort of independence; it is empowered to assert its own agency against other things. As such, it cannot be defined as an object, as its connection to the user is too intimate to differentiate. The difference between user and thing thus begins to fade. Our energy as active agents is funneled through things to particular parts of the world. Take the example of a mobile device. We can walk into a store or visit a website and see a multitude of styles, colors, sizes, and brands of devices, none of which have any particular meaning for us. They are dead material. As Heidegger tells us: "The vessel's thingness does not lie at all in the material of which it consists, but in the void that it holds."[52] In our case, the material of the device means nothing—we can lose our phone, break it, or have it stolen, but the part that matters is not the device itself but the information stored locally on the device and in applications, as well as the potential interactions the use of the device enables. The object-ness of the device—its screen and plastic shell—are not necessarily meaningless to users, as they can communicate through their physical design. Yet, it is the active engagement with the device that causes users to go beyond object-ness into thing-ness. The thingly qualities of the device extend beyond the physical attributes and into the space of meaning. Once we purchase the dead material of the device, we inject it with meaning by downloading applications, importing contacts, and using the device to accomplish other goals. The thing obtains meaning when we *go beyond it and bring it closer*. Assuming the ready-to-hand relationship of using an object in-order-to accomplish something else leads to its thingly qualities. Picking up and using something extends Dasein into a future state while still remaining wrapped up in the here and now.

Interacting with the device and using it to connect with other people, do our banking, conduct business, ward-off boredom, and get directions to physical places are all practices in bringing the device "closer" to us. This bringing-close, or gathering, is what creates a thing: "Clearly the jug stands as a vessel only because it has been brought to stand. This happened during, and happens by means of, a process of setting, of setting forth, namely, by producing the jug. The potter makes the earthen jug out of earth that he has specifically chosen and prepared for it."[53] Heidegger's example of the jug differs quite radically from our modern example of the mobile device. Why? For the jug, the craftsperson selects materials and molds them in a certain way to create a vessel, which a user then fills with water, and it thus becomes a thing. The gathering and molding of materials leads at least somewhat linearly to its use case. But the mobile device is not given its thing-ness by a craftsperson, or even a "designer," but rather by its users. The mobile device cannot stand on its own. The potential use cases are highly variable, and the user must define whether it is a device used in-order-to connect with other people, do our banking, conduct business, ward-off boredom, or get directions to physical places.

We'll end this chapter with a plea Heidegger makes—I believe—to designers:

> Our thinking has of course long been accustomed to understate the nature of the thing. The consequence, in the course of Western thought, has been that the thing is represented as an unknown X to which perceptible properties are attached. From this point of view, everything that already belongs to the gathering nature of this thing does, of course, appear as something that is afterward read into it.[54]

By neglecting the thing, philosophy has failed to address the nature of making. In addition to analyzing things already in existence, designers and philosophers should be coming together to examine the nature of the thing in the process of designing and making. Understanding the process of becoming—of the designer gathering material and meaning into a thing—

will be a central concern throughout the rest of this book, especially in terms of the relationship between the designer's encoded meaning and users' actual behaviors with the object.

Chapter 3
Design Thinking and Practice

Being a Designer

Now that we have looked a bit at what it means "to be" from a phenomenological perspective, we should spend some time on what it means "to be a designer." This section will map out the various aspects of this question, from the difference between "being" a designer and "thinking like" a designer, to whether the category of "designer" is even important, to the antinomies of design thinking, and the proposition that phenomenological philosophy is the next evolution of design thinking.

The main attraction to design thinking, and one that is often misunderstood, is that the "thinking" part extends far beyond a Cartesian model of the thinking subject. The designer is not one who theorizes about the world and acts based on speculation, as this is not representative of the human condition. Thinking inherently involves making. Externalization of thought *outside the head* is not only beneficial, but necessary. It is only through making that we are able to think. The creation of prototypes, for example, is not to simply create an object but rather to explore ideas in a physical space. The externalization of ideas is not linear; successful creation extends back to "thinking," thus linking the self and world, much like Heidegger's notion of Dasein. Design is a *Daseinerly* process, and Dasein is a designerly process (yes, I said it).

The fundamental question of this section revolves around the difference between "being" a designer and "thinking like" a designer, whether there is a difference—and if so, whether it matters. It is clear that there is a certain identity involved with being a designer, as Vilém Flusser says, "A shoemaker not only makes leather shoes; he also makes a shoemaker out of himself."[55] Our task here is trying to understand what "making a shoemaker out of himself" actually means. What is the significance of the title?

In a certain sense, we can begin to define the designer identity in the negative, or via what makes it different from science: "The scientist *discovers* a natural process or a natural law, but the engineer or designer *invents* a possible application or a new use suited to a particular product."[56] This idea of discovery and invention is crucial. A scientist examines the natural world and attempts to draw conclusions, extrapolating existing knowledge to provide a consistent notion of truth. A designer, on the other hand, examines the natural world and attempts to create future scenarios, eventually designing conditions for those scenarios—the key difference being analyzing *what is* (science) versus *what could be* (design). Given this broad definition, we might conclude that we are all designers, since at some point, we are all imagining future scenarios that make improvements on our current situation.

> Everyone can—and does—design. We all design when we plan for something new to happen, whether that might be a new version of a recipe, a new arrangement of the living room furniture, or a new layout of a personal web page. The evidence from different cultures around the world, and from designs created by children as well as by adults, suggests that everyone is capable of designing. So design thinking is something inherent within human cognition; it is a key part of what makes us human.[57]

Design exists not only in the beautiful buildings, utilitarian signage, or meaningful digital technologies that compete for our attention, but in the mundane daily tasks that alter our environment. Even reading this book might be considered a design activity, as it is affecting your point of view on the topics covered. By choosing this book over the millions of others available, you are deliberately shaping your perspective and orienting yourself toward these topics.

Richard Buchanan identifies this universal drive toward design in Aristotle's thinking:

For Aristotle, the differences among the various literary and constructive arts depend on a fundamental understanding of the human capacity to make, considered to be independent from the specialization of a particular art. All making is an integrative, synthetic activity. It is what he describes as an intellectual virtue: a reasoned state of the capacity to make, different from, but closely related to, the intellectual virtue that stands behind the theoretical sciences and the moral virtues that stand behind action. However, Aristotle also found it important to distinguish the element of forethought from the specific considerations and activities that are relevant to each kind of making. Forethought in making is a kind of universal art, in the sense that it is independent of any particular art of making and, therefore, able to range over all potential considerations and subjects that may enter into the making of this or that kind of product. Forethought is an 'architectonic' or 'master' art, concerned with discovery and invention, argument, and planning, and the purposes or ends that guide the activities of the subordinate arts and crafts. The element of forethought in making is what subsequently came to be known as design.[58]

The idea of forethought, then, is an aspect of humanity we can think of as an essential and universal component involved in the human capacity to design. This orientation toward the future—or the idea that Dasein exists ahead of itself—results in the capacity to design. If Heidegger is correct that Dasein is a goal-oriented phenomenon, then design is, as Cross also says, an inherent aspect of human cognition and existence. It is absurd to think humans go about in the world without affecting change—without purposefully crafting their own experiences—so it makes sense that we all design.

Still, there is something unique about "being a designer." And, even though he is not known for being a design theorist, Heidegger did devote much of his thinking to working out how to conceive of craft, making, and creation:

> [A cabinet maker's apprentice's] learning is not mere practice, to gain facility in the use of tools. Nor does he merely gather knowledge about the customary forms of the things he is to build. If he is to become a true cabinetmaker, he makes himself answer and respond above all to the different kind of wood and to the

shapes slumbering within the wood—to wood as it enters into man's dwelling with all the hidden riches of its nature. In fact, this relatedness to wood is what maintains the whole craft. Without that relatedness, the craft will never be anything but empty busywork, and occupation with it will be determined exclusively by business concerns. Every handicraft, all human dealings are constantly in that danger.[59]

The essence of craft for Heidegger is the relationship to materials. The craftsperson is not simply "making": they are in a continuous state of manipulating intimately familiar materials. Learning a craft is not only about learning the tools (this might be the least important part), but also orienting oneself toward the materials, becoming involved with them, and taking great care to use them in efficient, sustainable, and creative ways. The so-called "soft" skills are equally important as the "hard" skills. We see this constantly in experience design. As novice designers learn the craft, they often become obsessed with mastering the software tools involved in creating final deliverables. But as any seasoned experience designer knows, learning software is easy—the difficult part is knowing how to analyze user behavior, understand unsaid needs, and maintain a mindset based on designing for other people. Critical thinking skills are much more difficult to teach, and more difficult to learn, than hard skills. The difference often comes down to learning rules versus learning principles. In the former, rules might dictate how a piece of software or other design tool works, for example. It can be applied across contexts. In the latter, however, soft skills are taught through principles, frameworks, and styles of thinking that must be adapted to unique contexts. To add further complexity, experience designers rarely work with tangible material, as might an industrial designer. Their "material" is the experience, including all the messiness that comes with culture, understanding, and knowledge. "[H]andicraft is not the mere manipulation of tools, but the relatedness to wood."[60] Our job is to determine the relation to material when working with experiences.

We all design things, but a designer has a special relationship with and concern for materials. The designer also exhibits conscious and sustained care for design in a way the non-designers do not. That is to say, non-designers shape their world through everyday activity, but they do not apply the deep, involved thought that designers do (or should do). I want to propose that our capacity to design depends on two bodily capabilities: to speak and to use our hands. Hands are the means of making; the bodily sites of action. Derrida says "the hand cannot be spoken about without speaking of technics."[61] The act of making is quite literally tied to the body, and the hands serve the special function of not only grasping, but manipulating and shaping. Hands are involved in multitude of social relations, such as shaking hands as a symbolic means of sealing a contract, giving gifts, providing comfort to another person, stealing what is not ours, etc. Even further, hands are also the means of thinking. In old Cartesian models of the mind, the hand was simply the mechanical function of the mind; they carried out the work of the rational mind according to intentions one sought to affect in the world. Within phenomenology and newer forms of embodied cognition, however, thinking is carried out through bodily engagement facilitated through the hands. It's no coincidence that Heidegger's modes of interaction deal directly with the hands; the present-at-hand and ready-to-hand modes are associated with Dasein's ability to act with the world specifically through handedness.

In some of Heidegger's later work, he began to think more about the role of thinking with relation to craft:

> Perhaps thinking, too, is just something like building a cabinet. At any rate, it is a craft, a 'handicraft.' 'Craft' literally means the strength and skill in our hands. The hand is a peculiar thing. In the common view, the hand is part of our bodily organism. But the hand's essence can never be determined, or explained, by its being an organ which can grasp. Apes, too, have organs that can grasp, but they do not have hands. The hand is infinitely different from all grasping organs—paws, claws, or fangs—different by an abyss of essence. Only a being who can speak, that is, think, can have hands and can be handy in achieving works of handicraft [...] The hand reaches and extends, received and welcomes—and not just things: the hand extends itself, and receives its own welcome in the hands of others. The hand holds. The hand carries. The hand designs and signs, presumably because man is a sign.[62]

Heidegger identifies the hand as that which enables craft, but only through their interaction with other components of the human, such as thinking and speaking. Thought, speech, and the hands are coupled together to create our unique ability to design and make. This implies that craft needs these three components to emerge. One must think, speak, and use the hands in tandem in order to produce craft. In their ability to extend and receive, the hands also connect us to other people, and through this connection we are able to collaborate. The hand "designs and signs," implying that the hands create both functional and meaningful objects: they design things that function according to goals set forth by both designers and users, but they also create meaningful objects and systems that communicate a sense of significance for the interpreter.

We can see this type of thinking at work quite clearly as designers create and test prototypes. The handiwork of the designer is apparent in the creation of the prototype itself, and in the user's or test participant's handiwork in manipulating the object. When done well, prototyping will give designers a sense of both functionality and meaning; through user observation, designers will gain insight into usability issues on the functional level as well as interpretation issues on the level of meaning. So we see the prototype acting on three dimensions of craft as Heidegger articulates it. The hand creates the prototype; speech and the hand provide feedback; and thinking incorporates both.

A final point about the use of the hands deals with the idea of thrown-ness introduced in chapter 2. Heidegger posits that Dasein is thrown into the world and left to fend for itself, or cope with its surroundings. We might think of design as one way of coping. It is particularly convenient that the Dutch word *ost-werpen* can be read as un-throw, as Oosterling makes a very interesting point about design as the capacity to change current conditions—not necessarily in a Herbert Simon-influenced way, but simply to take an active role in existence. Through design, coping becomes a more active process of shaping our conditions. One of Sigmund Freud's famous insights on what he called the *fort-da* game (*fort* being German for "gone," and *da* being "here/there") is relevant here. Freud observed that when the child's mother left the room, he would become very upset, ostensibly assuming that his mother was gone forever. Eventually, the child picked up a spool of thread, holding the thread at one end and throwing the bobbin over the edge of his crib, exclaiming "*fort!*" He would then pull the bobbin back and yell "*da!*" Freud interpreted this game as the child's way of taking an active role in his mother's departure. Instead of accepting his thrown-ness into an unsatisfactory situation, he sought pleasure out of asserting some control over the situation. Similarly, we might think of designers as those who take an active role in their worldly situation, designing solutions for the things they deem undesirable. We are thrown into the world, but that doesn't mean we are forced into its current conditions. We all cope with the world, with its successes and failures—the title "designer" might simply be a term for someone who consciously and purposefully does so.

If objects are the means by which we relate to the world, speech is how we relate to each other. Speech is more than vocal communication—it extends to our ways of thinking. Much like Heidegger's notion of the hand facilitating thinking, speech also encompasses a method of thinking. We don't know what we think until we speak or make. These acts of articulating or making with the hands allow us to formulate the "inner" workings of the mind in physical/psychical space. Or perhaps, more precisely, speaking and making show us how thinking exists outside the self; how the division between self and world is not completely accurate. As Maurice Merleau-Ponty states, "Speech, in the speaker, does not translate ready-made thought, but accomplishes it."[63]

The idea of speech as a thinking mechanism should be familiar to designers. A central design research technique is user interviewing, which of course uses speech as its primary medium for communication. Throughout the interview process, researchers pay close attention to how participants articulate their needs, wants, desires, pain points—always with the caveat that what participants say is not necessarily what they really mean. The researcher's job is to interpret participants' responses and make sense of the stories they tell. Through interpretive and sense-making activities, researchers are able to form their own point of view on the topic at hand. That is, they act through the participant's speech to interpret and decode, eventually creating a holistic perspective on the research topic. The speech act is the means of truth-making. And conversely, participants will respond to questions and/or prompts with initial ready-made thoughts, as Merleau-Ponty might say, but will eventually create new senses of reality while speaking. For example, a participant might answer a question with a two-word answer. If the researcher is any good, they will probe for more information, at which point the participant is forced to "accomplish their thought" through speech; to use the speech act as a way to provoke the emergence of thought.

The deepest design research is informed by design ethnography, influenced by the anthropological method of observing culture. The ethnographer embeds themself into particular context and learns from observation and careful probing. The goal is to foster a deeply embodied relationship with research subjects: "Whether it is a question of another's body or my own, I have no means of knowing the human body other than that of living it, which means taking up on my own account the drama which is played out in it, and losing myself in it."[64] Ethnographic methods attempt to understand through experience. By inserting him/herself into a different context, the ethnographer is able to adapt and cope with that context in a similar manner as those who already exist in that context. These methods are often espoused because of their ability to generate empathy—a word that is beginning to be overused lately—but still has relevance for designers as a way to understand others.

Heidegger provides a perspective on empathy through the lens of being-with. If Dasein is being-there, then what is the nature of being-with others? Heidegger describes empathy as supposedly providing "the first ontological bridge from one's own subject, which is given proximally as alone, to the other subject, which is proximally quite closed off."[65] We can easily see how he would have a problem with a definition that posits a connection between two separate and distinct subjects, or the idea that one entity comes to understand an-other. One closed-off entity establishing a connection with another previously unattainable entity does not fit with the praxical, situated nature of Dasein. We might, therefore, rethink empathy as something that "does not first constitute Being-with; only on the basis of Being-with does 'empathy' become possible: it gets its motivation from the unsociability of the dominant modes of Being-with."[66]

Being-with, then, provides the conditions of possibility for empathy. Empathy is not something we *do* but is rather a consequence of our being-with others. In this way, the conscious generation of empathy through design research methods and problem-framing is a conscious enactment of our being-with others. Empathy exists everywhere and at any time we demonstrate understanding for others. Empathy within design is simply a (supposedly) more systematic and reliable means of creating the conditions for empathy to be its most effective. This purposeful generation of empathy can feel contrived at times, but as Gallagher and Zahavi convincingly argue, "there is no pure third-person perspective, just as there is no view from nowhere."[67] So empathy becomes the option to establish a point of view based on our authentic being-with.

If being-with is a central component of Dasein, and empathy is a phenomenon that emerges out of being-with, then a key question for designers is how to provoke the emergence of empathy. What are the necessary conditions of empathetic responses? I'm not sure we can answer that question here, but I do want to claim that speech is the medium of empathy insofar as it facilitates understanding. In the design research setting, participants are engaged through speech as a primary means of establishing connection and gathering information. Through questions and probing, the researcher is able to extract information and hear stories about the topic at hand, hopefully generating a sense of empathetic understanding for the participants. The most rigorous research methods will use a combination of interviews and behavioral observation to compare the difference between real behavior and accounts of behavior. We should remember that empathy does not always need to be a positive phenomenon; we might discover that participants lie, and that act of lying may establish empathetic understanding in the same way a positive account can. So the process of empathetic understanding in design is a conscious and purposeful way of everyday being-with.

What is interesting about speech in the design process, however, is that speech and non-speech can operate in a similar manner. That is, while speaking to research participants can elicit information, aid sense-making, and facilitate empathy, the lack of speech in design research can also facilitate empathy. Examples of this phenomenon can be seen in pure observational studies in which vicarious understanding is achieved through observation and reflection, or through a researcher practicing active listening in an interview. It is natural to fill awkward silences, but researchers who train themselves to listen more than they speak can discover deeper insights: "Paradoxically, the manner of speaking in which empathy is made explicit is a privation—keeping silent and listening. In keeping silent we are open to the other and the other's way of being [...] The optimal form of speech in which empathy is articulated is as empathic listening."[68]

At this point, we might question the nature of empathy through speech as a necessary part of the design process. Certainly, Heidegger had his doubts about the nature of empathy even though he declared the intimate interrelation between being-there and being-with. Is it inauthentic, then, to assume a sense of understanding for another person or group of people?

This question is, of course, both provocative and borderline nonsensical. Design might be the most meaningful demonstration of how empathy plays itself out as a conscious phenomenon. That is, design as a field relies on empathy, not simply to fuel the design process but also because the nature of design inserts a gap between those who make and those who use. Empathy, at least, ideally, helps bridge that gap.

The Nigel Cross quote near the beginning of this chapter linking design to everyday manipulation of the environment suggests that the act of design is a universal human trait; depending on the definition of "design" one uses, however, this statement might not be correct. In a certain sense, perhaps it is more accurate to say "we all participate in craft" rather than "we all design things." Certainly, we all change our environment: alterations of recipes, the organization of a medicine cabinet, body modification, etc. But rarely do we change our environment for the sake of others. And this gets us to the difference between design and craft.

> In traditional, craft-based societies the conception, or 'designing', of artefacts is not really separate from making them; that is to say, there is usually no prior activity of drawing or modelling before the activity of making the artefact. For example, a potter will make a pot by working directly with the clay, and without first making any sketches or drawings of the pot. In modern, industrial societies, however, the activities of designing and of making artefacts are usually quite separate. The process of making something does not normally start before the process of designing it is complete.[69]

And further:

> Artisans, as it were, 'designed' artifacts in the course of constructing them, so that making seldom involved anything like a separate moment of thinking out or planning beforehand, but proceeded as intuitive trial-and-error fabrication, letting oneself be guided by materials and tradition, and even by personal relationships in the community.[70]

We touched on these points in chapter 2 and revisited them earlier in this section, but we are now in a much better place to articulate the differences between craft and design. Tony Fry sums it up quite well: "Craft is a material practice of caring in making that folds into the maker and the made."[71] Design is a particularly modern phenomenon. We can classify craft as, among other things, an act of creation in which designer, maker, and user are the same, and which allows the maker to bring about or reveal certain qualities through the skillful combination, interrelation, and deep relationship to materials.

> Prior to the rise of modern technology design was hidden or embedded in the craft of making, which was itself a characteristic

activity of Dasein. Artisans in their particularities of body, place, and history were at one and the same time those who conceived or imagined artifacts and went to work to fabricate them. Aboriginally they were also the users. Artisans in wooded geographies worked with wood, wood growing there (not elsewhere); artisans living in rock-rich landscapes worked with stone, stone quarried there (and not elsewhere). They worked also with the strength and skills of their own bodies, and within the traditions of their peoples or cultures.[72]

Mitcham emphasizes local materials and the work of the body as core components of craft. Craftspeople worked with what they had: material in their immediate environment and their own bodily capability. Contrast that with modern design, and we see designers working with physical material from literally anywhere in the world, digital "material" we make ourselves, and almost always working through the power of a machine. We can see now that Heidegger's anxiety toward modern technology (covered in the previous chapter) was not necessarily aimed at technology itself, but rather at the *design* of technology. The disconnect between Dasein, its body, and the immediate environment we find in the design process caused Heidegger to worry about things like river dams and the shoring up of energy. Once we broke the intimate connection between maker and user that we find in craft, design came into being as that which both establishes and attempts to close that gap. What Heidegger failed to recognize, however, is the capacity for design to mediate the thrown-ness of Dasein and establish a sense of activity within the world.

What we call "design" is in part a product of the Industrial Revolution. One aspect of the movement from craft to design is division of labor. We can observe this division across industries, perhaps most pronounced in automobile manufacturing, where Ford became famous and highly profitable (at least for a while) by compartmentalizing the work of car manufacturing into specific parts. The assembly line allowed workers to concentrate their efforts on discrete tasks—filling a bucket of bolts, bending a piece of metal, fetching tires, etc.—instead of worrying about entire systems. Cars could be designed and manufactured, thus splitting the planning out of a system and the discrete tasks involved in creating the physical object. In other words, labor became compartmentalized and efficiency-obsessed. We saw movements like Taylorism attempting to maximize labor efforts to an extreme, and lean manufacturing reducing waste to keep up with Ford. The division of labor during the Industrial Revolution has become "both the great strength and the Achilles' heel of our industrial society."[73] This division is a strength because it has resulted in some major advances in how we build products and create jobs. It is also, however, a weakness because it causes an immense amount of waste, from unproductive meetings, to miscommunications, to apathetic middle managers.

Experience designers have been dealing with these strengths and weaknesses for many years now, either from nonstop evangelizing within large companies or spending so much time documenting their designs that they have no time to actually *design*. The resulting angst comes to a head in trends like "unicornism," or the fetishization of the designer who can think in terms of systems and interfaces; who can seamlessly move from research to synthesis to design execution to testing to code—an extremely rare creature who often *can* perform these functions, but usually only excels at one. Unicornism proponents often cite the waste involved in the division of design labor, cost effectiveness in having a few "maker-generalists" over large teams, and the growing implosion of design and development practices. While it might be true that dividing labor among researchers, interface designers, experience designers, developers, etc. could very well be foreign to readers not long after this book is published, I do want to quickly bring up some points on unicornism.

One might view a movement like this as a regression to the craftsperson: individuals who work on a product from beginning to end, seeing it through from conception to tangible reality. And not only "seeing it through" but actively creating the various parts. The individual in this situation looks a lot more like a craftsperson than a designer (according to our definitions so far), especially in Lean frameworks and startups in which "upfront design" is minimized or eliminated. However, the movement from craft to design in the Industrial Revolution also ushered a dramatic increase in complexity to the products and services we use everyday. The unicorn designer, a pure generalist, is simply not equipped to deal with this complexity. They are great at making relatively simple products, where it makes a lot of sense to consolidate labor into one person rather than hire a team. But complex design projects that require a deep understanding of people call for a certain amount of specialty and rigor.

In the end, this debate goes back to care. The division of labor in design has resulted in the perception that designers who specialize in one component of the process become complacent—much like an assembly line worker might simply want to ride out their shift and go home, or an office worker who puts in eight hours in the cubicle to be free the rest of the day. What these divided labor workers have in common is a lack of care or concern with the outcomes of their work. This is well-documented, of course, by Karl Marx in his notion of alienation. For our purposes, however, we can concentrate on how to keep designers involved throughout the process of designing and developing complex products and services. "Care has to be designed into being, and craft is the means by which this can be done."[74] Returning to Henk Oosterling's point on design as the practice of "un-throwing," we use design to exert an active stance toward the world and care for the outcomes we provoke. And through this care of designing, we come to know the world. *Techne*, or the craft/hand-work in which designers take part, is both an act of making and an act of knowing.[75] Being a designer involves the preservation of the connections between making, caring, knowing, and understanding.

Thinking Like a Designer

We now turn our attention to design thinking as a means of explaining how designers think. One can argue that the roots of design thinking go back to the 1960s with Herbert Simon's *Sciences of the Artificial*, or perhaps even earlier to 1940 with Harold van Doren's *Industrial Design: A Practical Guide to Product Design and Development*. Work continued through the 60s onward with contributions from a long list of design theorists and practitioners. In the 90s, we saw a transition from design thinking as a mostly academic focus to a business-oriented mindset with work from IDEO—a global design consultancy that used design thinking as their process framework and as a means of facilitating communication within large organizations. They were able to articulate how non-designers often think like designers.

The epistemology of design revolves around the difference between how designers think in contrast to science and the humanities. Nigel Cross sums up the key differences quite nicely:

The phenomenon of study in each culture is
- in the sciences: the natural world
- in the humanities: human experience
- in design: the artificial world

The appropriate methods in each culture are

- in the sciences: controlled experiment, classification, analysis
- in the humanities: analogy, metaphor, evaluation
- in design: modelling, pattern-formation, synthesis

The values of each culture are
- in the sciences: objectivity, rationality, neutrality, and a concern for 'truth'
- in the humanities: subjectivity, imagination, commitment, and a concern for 'justice'
- in design: practicality, ingenuity, empathy, and a concern for 'appropriateness'[76]

As we can see, scientists study the natural world through controlled experiments, aiming at Truth through objectivity and neutrality. The sciences are concerned with *what is*, relying on valid experiments and analysis to deduce truth. The humanities, on the other hand, are less concerned with truth than interpretation. They seek to discover the nuances of human experience by using metaphorical analysis and individual interpretation to tell stories about how we experience the world. Finally, design seeks to determine *what could be* by creating models, observing behavior, and discovering patterns. Phenomenology, of course, falls cleanly within the humanities category; its core topic is that of human experience, and metaphor and analogy are its means of articulating *what seems to be*. Our concern in this book is the bridge between humanities, particularly phenomenology, and design. Where do these categories overlap? And how might that overlap be valuable to each? How can we use phenomenology to think about futures?

There are many definitions of design thinking, but perhaps the most famous comes from IDEO. A few variations exist, but most focus on three key areas: business, technology, and people. We might say that design thinking as applied to business problems involves a mediation of technological capabilities, opportunity for profit, and the needs of users. In its ideal state, design thinking creates a harmony among these three pillars of design. But what we might colloquially think of as design thinking usually has to do with ideas of "creativity" or "innovation," the creation of new opportunities seemingly from nothing. The cognitive component to creativity is abductive thinking—the cognitive component that allows us to think about possible futures as opposed to explaining the present. If we can pinpoint the key characteristic of design thinking from an epistemological point of view, it would be that designers rely on abductive thinking to determine *what could be*.

Logic is usually explained through deduction or induction— deduction as the logic of absolute truth, and induction as the logic of scientific reasoning:

> Deductive reasoning is the reasoning of formal logic: if a is the same as b, and b is the same as c, then a is the same as c. Inductive reasoning is the logic of science: you observe all the swans in a given region; you note that each and every swan is white; you form the rule that 'all swans are white' (which you may find is false when you move to another region and discover some black swans). Abduction is the logic of design: you are asked to design a telephone for mature people; you know that mature people like clarity and elegant forms and colours; you propose a design with a smoothly contoured, soft-white case and clear, black buttons (one of many possible proposals for achieving clarity and elegance).[77]

As we can see, design must go beyond an understanding of *what is* and extend itself toward future states of being—that is, how can we frame existing states to reveal opportunities for improvement? Deduction and induction mostly look toward the past and present, while abduction orients itself to the future, and is therefore an inherently individual and intuitive act—individual because the interpretive act fuels designers' conclusions, and intuitive because empirical evidence is not always in play.

There is a certain sense of emergence in design thinking—the infamous "aha!" moment in which research insights come together in a perfect solution. Many designers live for this moment, constantly chasing the perfect synthesis of insight and execution. This moment, however, is extremely rare, as abductive thinking, which ostensibly leads to this moment, is problematic:

> Abduction acts as inference or intuition, and is directly aided and assisted by personal experience. Yet the personal experience need not be with the specific subject matter of the design problem. The abduction itself can be driven by any design or cultural patterns that act as an argument from best explanation. As described by Peirce, 'The abductive suggestion comes to us like a flash. It is an

act of insight, although extremely fallible insight. It is true that the different elements of the hypothesis were in our minds before; but it is the idea of putting together what we had never before dreamed of putting together which flashes the new suggestion before our contemplation.'[78]

Designing for future states forces designers to rely on their individual, fallible experience. Design thinking, I would argue, attempts to mediate the cognitive biases, fallacies, and logical leaps that come with individual or even collaborative introspection. It does so by constantly reflecting on itself; creating prototypes of ideas in order to examine how objects operate in praxis; and undergoing constant iteration and critique. So design thinking as a process becomes a means for ensuring the individual style of design does not result in hyper-introspective "creative geniuses." Design thinking is a method to help designers stay somewhere in the middle of purely intuitive thinking and purely analytical thinking.

There is the sense within abductive thinking that a designer's work is embodied in the acts of thinking and making. In other words, designers produce objects (final or prototypical) that are used to reflect on the process of thinking, or we might say, become part of the thinking process itself. It demonstrates how closely related thinking and making are. Thinking through the body becomes an important part of how we conceive of design; it is not an act of thinking and then making, but rather it is thinking through making—a process that only comes to fruition through know-how. The embodied practice of knowing-how, as the core component of making, is difficult to explain. For example, musicians are especially aware of the difference between reading sheet music and the act of actually playing the instrument. The former is a reflective, almost present-at-hand type of relationship, whereas the latter is a fully embodied, ready-to-hand act of know-how. Expertise, both in music and in design, comes from the ability to move in and out of embodied states, as Cameron Tonkinwise explains:

> Know-how resists articulation in two ways. Firstly, know-how becomes activated by being disarticulated. If I learn a task firstly as a set of explicit rules, becoming more adept at a task means no longer having to use such explicit rules; discrete actions get chunked into larger activities; and then activity series get integrated into single acts. Expertise means being able to focus on ends

rather than means; the know-how takes care of things without requiring explicit attention. Importantly, the integrative disarticulation that is the acquiring of expertise is not one-way; faced with a problem or a surprising situation, what differentiates an authentic expert from a mere task automator, is an ability to re-disaggregate the act, articulating each component action for scrutiny. Secondly, know-how is procedurally integrated via the body. What minds the actions comprising an act, allowing the expert to focus on the end rather than the means, or even on something else entirely, is their body. Hubert Dreyfus, amongst others, drawing on Heidegger and Merleau-Ponty has made clear that even purely mental expert tasks have an embodied aspect, a felt sense of whether they are 'on track' as they proceed. Evidence is the sense of excitement and anxiety that we feel in our stomachs when an act being learned goes (publicly) right or wrong. Learning to do something expertly means getting a feel for the normal operation of that process, so that the interrelated senses of the body remain alert to any out-of-ordinary occurences. So, not only are expert level skills deliberately tacit-ed actions, but they are tacit-ed by being turned into wholistic bodily sensations. These skills can be articulated, for teaching for example, but such articulations involve not just remembering the actions that comprise an act, but also dis-membering how those acts have been efficiently embodied; highly subjective feelings must be made sharable.[79]

Design expertise is measured by the ability to perform embodied, or in Tonkinwise's terms, "tacit-ed," activities while maintaining the ability to zoom out of the experience and reflect on it. It means articulating aspects of design that have been fully embodied, much in the same way as a music teacher must explain and demonstrate skills that s/he does not reflect upon while in the act. In other words, designers are to reflect on the abductive thinking process and draw communicable insights from it, but only when the process itself is over. If reflection is timed incorrectly, it breaks the embodied nature of abduction. For example, in design workshops I run—of which abductive thinking is a key component—participants sketch for a certain amount of time, then present and critique one another for a certain amount of time. This highly controlled method aims to counter the free-for-all nature of many brainstorming sessions in which there is no differentiation between abduction, induction, deduction, embodiment, and reflection.

The preceding discussion on abduction leads us to a brief summary of design thinking as a process. What is perhaps most interesting about design thinking in the context of phenomenology is that it does not differentiate between the "thinking" part and the "making" part. Thinking can only be completed through the act of making, and similarly making is only possible through thinking. This dialectic allows us to push past arguments that design thinking is merely a thought experiment or a detached theory of design—it opens the door for articulating how the act of designing informs reflection on design. While design thinking is unique in its use of abductive thinking, it is not exclusive to this type of logic. That is, design thinking also makes use of inductive and deductive thinking, or at least it attempts to; we simply tend to not dwell on them, as abduction, or the "creative process," tends to be more interesting to designers. However, showing how all types of thinking contribute to design is necessary to draw important connections between design, humanities, and sciences.

We can break down design thinking into four component parts: 1) empathy for alternate contexts; 2) framing of problems and opportunities; 3) ideation of multiple solutions; and 4) validation of executions. There are many ways to frame a design thinking process. This is just one.

1) Empathy for alternate contexts

Design thinking acknowledges the vast amount of cognitive biases that influence designers. Designers, therefore, use research methodologies in order to resolve biased intuition and observable phenomena. For example, a designer might believe that banking has become inconvenient and customers might be better served through mobile technologies, which in turn will save money and create new revenue opportunities for banks. With this thought in mind, the next move is to observe bank customers to determine if they experience the same problems and to discover other ways that traditional banking is inconvenient. There are many possibilities for what the designer might learn during research, including: 1) others experience the same problems; 2) others experience the same problems but in different ways; 3) problems identified are idiosyncratic; 4) something in-between the previous three. Research methods aim to understand different contexts so a designer can validate and/or add new perspective to an existing hypothesis.

The end goal of research is to discover *what is,* making research a predominantly inductive act. This is a lofty goal for design, as its units of measurement are behavioral, qualitative, and therefore not easily quantified. But that's okay. Qualitative design methods aim to describe motivations, cognitive patterns, and experiences, none of which can be measured in the same way as quantifiable information, such as demographics—at least not in a way that is valuable for design. Human-centered designers are mostly interested in experience, which can only be measured qualitatively.

2) Framing of problems and opportunities

Once research observations are collected, designers frame problems and opportunities to help concentrate on what they believe to be most important. In the previous example concerning mobile banking, imagine researcher-designers found that bank customers were particularly frustrated with complicated ATM interfaces, long lines at teller booths, and fees associated with checking accounts. The designer's job is to expand upon observations and attempt to determine *why* these are problems, and, once they have a sense of causal factors, how to concentrate time, people, and resources on solving the most important problem. In this example, designers might not be able to affect fees on checking accounts, but they might be able to better communicate why those fees exist and how to avoid them. They might also find out that the reason for long lines has to do with poor layout in physical banks, or that a particular type of bank customer tends to use physical banks more than others. The bank might be in a lower income area, with customers who are more concerned with and more prone to overdraft fees. The list can go on.

Framing problems and opportunities is a sense-making task. It involves finding meaning in a vast amount of observational data. The research process generates a wealth of findings, and framing attempts to make sense of them and develop a point of view. For example, a confusing ATM interface might be confusing for a number of reasons—it might not have enough international language support; it might have poor information architecture and customers cannot make sense of how to perform certain functions; it might be in a sunny outdoor area that produces glare on the screen; etc. Some of these problems have simple solutions, while others are quite complex. Framing is the interpretive process by which designers determine complexity and how to deal with it. Given its interpretive nature, framing has much in common with the humanities and intuitive thinking. Just like a literary critic or philosopher might take qualitative, textual material as their point of focus by reading and interpreting the text, forming an opinion, and arguing a position, a designer, on the other hand, takes research findings as material to argue an opinion based on individual experience. In this way, framing in design is not terribly different from having a point of view on a news story, or interpreting the meaning of a novel.

3) Ideation of multiple solutions

The ideation process is the stage within design thinking that most directly deals with abductive thinking. Once teams have identified problems and opportunities, they work collaboratively to design as many solutions as possible before determining which is the most appropriate for the problem space. For example, if designers discover that the information architecture of the bank's ATMs is poorly designed, they might come up with multiple alternate design solutions, exploring many different possibilities before choosing the preferred one. They might re-categorize information, create new transitions between screens, etc.

This focus on creating possibilities is at the heart of abductive thinking. Traditional, business-focused brainstorming might set aside an hour or so to quickly explain a problem space to a group of people with varying levels of familiarity, "throw some ideas at the wall" in a free-for-all manner, and then make a decision on what to design. I'm sure most readers can relate to this process and its inherent downfalls, so we won't concentrate on them here other than to point out that this type of brainstorming usually results in premature convergence—teams decide on a solution (or it is decided for them) before they are able to fully explore possibilities. Design thinking attempts to mediate premature convergence through ideation methods that focus on flattening hierarchies, maintaining proper timing and balance between sketching sessions, presenting, and critiquing. It also attempts to mediate abductive thinking about *what could be* with *what is feasible* and *what is desirable*.

4) Validation of executions

Finally, validation serves as the most analytical aspect of design thinking. Designers produce sketches, determine which are most appropriate, and prototype some of them to test in real settings, with the goal of validating or invalidating their executions. Prototypes can take many forms—from simple paper to modeled environments to mostly functioning products.

Artifacts put to use in real contexts reveal themselves to be useful, meaningful, usable, and all permutations in between. Allowing users to engage in praxical use enables designers to observe objects in use, rather than theoretical objects in the process of being designed. Prototyping is the design equivalent of phenomenological praxis theory; the prototyped artifact acts as the medium for acting-through, and allows the designer to observe behavior from a present-at-hand position. Somewhat similar to empathizing with multiple contexts, the aim here is often to empirically determine the artifact's value in the context of a design problem, but more often than not designers are dealing with interpretive methods. Methods such as usability testing can often feel quite scientific and analytical, but designers are still relying on interpretive techniques tied to their individual experience.

The preceding discussions on abductive thinking and design thinking as a means of informing process put us in a position to go deeper into the relationship between phenomenology and experience design. At the center of this connection is a breakdown of dualistic notions of thinking and making (and problems and solutions as we'll see in the next chapter). Probably the most influential study of the thinking-making relationship is detailed in Donald Schön's work. Schön sought to explain his idea of reflective practice through stories about how design practitioners and other professionals think while acting—that is, there is an embodied sense of performance, similar to that of the craftsperson, found in many professional activities in which the practitioner exhibits a reflexive movement between thinking and acting. In this particularly phenomenological move, Schön was able to link theory and practice into a single praxical movement. Even though Schön was not a phenomenologist himself, his work (among others we will cover in the upcoming chapters) has laid the groundwork for thinking about a phenomenological perspective on the next evolution of design thinking.

Design Thinking and Phenomenology

Our account of design thinking thus far has focused on thinking like, acting like, and being a designer from a phenomenological perspective. Hopefully this examination helped elucidate some of the nuances in design, as well as articulate some connections between phenomenology and design. Pushing this connection a bit further, I want to argue that a phenomenological point of view is the next evolution of design thinking—that is, the study of human experience must be an epistemological concentration for designers, and design must be viewed as a means of experience bringing itself into existence.

One of the main claims of design thinking is that, as a process, it helps solve wicked problems. As opposed to a tame problem—which is relatively easily defined and understood—a wicked problem is characterized by its defiance of comprehensive definition, the systemic involvement of multiple forces, its inherent complexity, and a lack of a clear end state.[80] Common examples of wicked problems include global climate change, world hunger, and natural resource depletion. Design thinking claims to be a framework for working through these problems and for understanding the component parts and formulating solutions appropriate to a context. What design thinking frameworks often lack, however, is a rigorous approach to studying the human experience. Research methodologies are excellent ways to enact theoretical models of human experience, but more focused, experiential models do not exist within design theory. Wicked problems call for the most holistic of design approaches, including a deep concern for behavioral and cognitive components of an experience, while phenomenology provides the reflective components of the interaction between these components. When we think and behave, there is an experiential aspect that is missing in most design theory that can be explained by phenomenology.

Johansson-Sköldberg, Woodilla, and Çetinkaya explain the broad strokes evolution of design thinking as such:

1. Design and designerly thinking as the creation of artefacts (Simon, 1969).
2. Design and designerly thinking as a reflexive practice (Schön, 1983).
3. Design and designerly thinking as a problem-solving activity (Buchanan, 1992 based on Rittel and Webber, 1973).
4. Design and designerly thinking as a way of reasoning/making sense of things (Lawson, 2006 [1980]; Cross, 2006, 2011).
5. Design and designerly thinking as creation of meaning (Krippendorff, 2006).[81]

When tracking design thinking all the way back to the late 1960s with Herbert Simon, we see a concentration on specific artifacts of design, and how design seeks to improve the human experience by pushing it to a preferred state. Donald Schön[82] picks up the conversation with his famous study of practitioners and the phenomenon of reflective practice, showing how professionals enact thinking through making. Rittel and Webber[83] (mentioned above) explain how design thinking deals with wicked problems involving multiple contingencies. We then progress to a concern for how designers think in contrast to scientists or theorists in the humanities with Lawson[84] and Cross.[85] Finally, Krippendorff[86] shows how design thinking extends beyond designer and user to create a sense of meaning through the designed objects.

To continue this line of thinking, I want to argue that design thinking is a phenomenological endeavor. Phenomenology can play a twofold role it its relationship to design thinking: 1) Phenomenology provides a basis for design's claims about the human experience. The process of design thinking always deals with people and their experiences, and phenomenology gives a means of exploring experience. 2) Design is the process of enacting the human experience through products and services. Concepts from phenomenology will provide new perspectives on design as well as introduce new ones.

The overview of Heidegger's thought has so far given us new insights in what it means to design, to be a designer, and to understand others. As we move through the upcoming chapters, we will return to Heidegger's thoughts on praxis as the means by which humans engage with the world and technology as a mediator of actions. We will further examine the nature of handedness and making as frameworks for design processes. The process of abductive thinking and orienting oneself as a designer will become clearer with modern applications. And finally, we will see new ways of concerning ourselves with end users and the empathetic process of understanding. Using Heidegger's work as a basis, we will shift focus from phenomenology to a more modern version of post-phenomenology, which emphasizes the role of embodiment, specific technological devices, and technology as a mediating force.

Chapter 4
The Problem-Solution Paradox

The Paradox of Design

The point of transition between phenomenology and post-phenomenology in this discussion on design rests on a paradox: the problem-solution paradox.

Design thinking has attempted to formalize a human-centered design process that gives equal weight to user, business, and technology concerns.[87] As a process, it works toward a deep understanding of human behavior through research methods such as design ethnography, and framing a problem space within research findings. With a problem area isolated, design thinking applies structured creativity to take advantage of abductive thinking, create multiple solutions, and decide which is most appropriate. The best solutions are then prototyped and tested. As we have seen in the previous chapter, design thinking has its roots in academic design research and related fields.

A somewhat related offshoot known as "lean startup"[88] emphasizes a cyclical approach to design. Teams work to identify assumptions they have about users and the market, then build a prototype specifically designed to test one or more of those assumptions. If assumptions are validated, teams move on to test other assumptions; if assumptions are invalidated, teams rethink their initial premises and create new prototypes. Lean startup originates from lean manufacturing and systems thinking, but tones down much of this history to speak to a business-minded audience.

Both processes have been successful in getting designers to think more about users as driving factors for design decisions, and to use prototypes to enact real interactions in order to understand them in context. But there is a tension that each of these methodological frameworks attempts to overcome, and ultimately fails to do so. This tension is something inherent in all design disciplines, and, despite its ubiquity, defies traditional conceptions of solutions. It is the meta example of a wicked problem.

Both frameworks illustrate a paradox. What I like to call the problem-solution paradox states that we cannot think about solutions until we understand the problem, and we cannot understand a problem until we think about solutions.

The first part of the paradox is familiar. Good design processes attempt to clearly define a problem space before designing solutions, thus cutting down on wasted time and resources. Designers move linearly from understanding to framing to ideation to validation, ensuring rigor at each step to inform the next. However, there are issues with this linear course. First, it assumes that there is a "final answer" at the end of the "understanding" phase, and, once we find it, we can design for it. This would be fine if design were an analytical task in which all problems have solutions. But as we have seen, design is abductive in the sense that designers are not looking for Truth but rather the many truths that might be appropriate to specific contexts. We should, therefore, resist the urge to seek final answers. Second, the linear approach assumes that designers are able to understand a problem space as divorced from potential solutions. Although this might be true in part, it does not account for the complexity of behavior. The linear movement from problem to solution does not leave room for exploring the effects of solutions on the system for which they are designed. It is a theoretical stance—even with the most rigorous contextual research, most findings are theoretical in nature.

The second part of the paradox attempts to solve these issues, but does so by simply reversing them. It allows the exploration of possibilities via prototypes, but in the process it eliminates valuable insights that come from theoretical work. Using solutions to understand a problem space is a purely practical approach—the creation of entities in a system elucidates the nature of that system. While this approach sounds good on the surface, it can easily be interpreted as a means to eliminate the complex parts of design: observing complex behavioral systems, and understanding cognitive patterns beyond what someone consciously says.

We can see how design thinking might respond to the paradox by asserting that the process is not as linear as it might seem. Designers frequently rethink problem spaces and return to early phases based on what they learn in the latter ones. And, lean design simply claims that using prototypes to explore possibilities accounts for a praxis-based design process, thus eliminating the need to spend time on upfront research. Still, neither of these arguments is valid, as they both only account for half of the paradox. Lean and design thinking are used as examples here, not simply because they are currently en vogue, but because they tacitly attempt to address the paradox identified here, and their underlying assumptions extend far beyond their processes.

What the problem-solution paradox identifies is not new to philosophy—these paradoxical relationships exist across philosophical and even scientific approaches. It was first alluded to in Rittel and Webber's examination,[89] and called out again by Kees Dorst.[90] Within phenomenology, Heidegger's examination of art[91] concentrated on the hermeneutic circle: an idea from linguistics and textual interpretation, which maintains that an understanding of a text depends on each word, and an understanding of each word depends on the text. In other words, parts depend on the whole, and the whole depends on the parts. Heidegger maintained that art does not have "thingly" characteristics in the sense of other objects and concepts we can point to or define. Instead, art is dependent on a vast system of individual pieces of artwork and their artists. We cannot refer to a piece of art without also referring to other pieces of art and their creators. Therefore, we are left with the impossibility of referring to a piece of art without the whole, and the whole of art without the pieces. In linguistics, Ferdinand de Saussure proposes that signs have no meaning in themselves but rather derive meaning based on their relationship to one another and in the differences among individuals.[92] Within what Saussure describes as a "chain of signification," signs are constantly referring to other individual signs and to the linguistic system as a whole. And finally, Donald Schön describes the design process as a conversation with the situation, in which designers are constantly taking cues from the environment and introducing new variables into the same environment.[93]

All these paradoxes stem from non-dualist philosophies. If we were to remain complacent with dualism, we might say a painting is simply a manifestation of art—signs point to things and their inherent meaning, and design is simply the manifestation of a designer's intent. However, these dualist points of view ignore the connections between wholes and parts. Similarly, the problem-solution paradox points out that a linear movement from problem to solution is overly simplistic, and despite the complexity and paradoxical nature of the alternative, we need a different way to characterize how design deals with wholes and parts. So as we continue to articulate problem spaces, we will realize that introducing solutions into those spaces does not necessarily "solve" the problem, but merely changes the conditions in which the problem exists. Sometimes this is enough to improve the overall experience; sometimes it is not. The important thing to remember is that without a one-to-one relationship between problem and solution, designers are not in a place to introduce solutions. Instead, they influence systems with the end goal of influencing the experience of that system.

The rest of this chapter, and to a certain extent the rest of this book, will be dedicated to further examining the problem-solution paradox and how we might reframe it through the lens of phenomenology. The key questions include: How do we effectively use potential solutions as means of understanding problem spaces? And, how do we take a problem space, in its constantly evolving motion, as the starting point for designing these solutions?

Questioning Design Dualisms

The difficulty of the problem-solution dichotomy is that design is not always about solving problems. Many design theorists like to preserve a sort of anti-capitalist, utopian version of design in which we only create things that solve an important and identified need. While this view is certainly beneficial—and we need people to continue striving for that ideal—the truth is that much of the designed world is driven by profit. Thus, many designs do not necessarily solve a problem but rather meet a previously unmet need in the market, or introduce a product that people believe they cannot live without through the magic of marketing. The primary example of this latter effect is, of course, the release of the iPhone in 2007. The device itself was a great design success, but even more so, the iTunes store expanded beyond the device to create an entire ecosystem of applications and services under the Apple umbrella. Apple very quickly created a service environment that consumers wanted to buy into, and once they did, it became easy to continue purchasing add-ons, other devices, new software versions, etc. In the end, Apple was not solving a problem; rather, they were meeting a previously-unarticulated need for an internet-connected device and a network of associated services that drastically simplified the experience (although not without detriment).

Nonetheless, the problem-solution dichotomy is convenient as long as we remember two things: 1) Problems are not always user-centric. Design teams can also work on business problems such as low sales, increased competition, etc. In a user-centric design process, designers would work to find an overlap between business and user needs, but this is not always the case. 2) The problem-solution dichotomy is not a dichotomy. Only under the most strict dualist frameworks are problems and solutions viewed as antithetical and relationally linear. And, only in these dualist models do designers identify a problem and apply a solution to it. The non-dualist point of view I will argue in this chapter calls for a more open perspective—one that sees design as more complex than a problem-solution equation. I will aim to show that problems and solutions are wrapped up in one another, and that we can only understand one through the lens of the other.

Other design theorists[94] have identified the problematic separation between problems and solutions, but have not applied their thinking to experience design. I think that within modern experience design, we see a heightened concentration on dualism, as many projects are commercially-backed by clients who become hyper-concentrated on a solution (or even have a solution in mind before design begins). Design agencies, then, become focused on reinforcing what their client wants rather than the best solution. The aim here is to recontextualize the problem-solution relationship within experience design to decrease this urge.

Quoting architect Richard MacCormac, Nigel Cross remarks: "'I don't think you can design anything just by absorbing information and then hoping to synthesise it into a solution. What you need to know about the problem only becomes apparent as you're trying to solve it.' This confirms a view that the design brief is not a specification for a solution, but the starting point for an exploration."[95] MacCormac points out the false dualism that pervades design: formulating a problem space is not a step in a process but rather an emergent, constantly evolving, reflective activity. One does not simply move from problem to solution; designers discover the problem space, or at least evolve the problem space, in the process of creating solutions. This is the combination of thinking and making. If we are to entertain this idea that problem and solution emerge together, we are abandoning more traditional, dualist design philosophies. The Cartesian perspective would hold that the designer removes him/herself from the design situation in order to more "objectively" analyze it by spending time planning, assessing, and mapping out intentions that are later executed in a different phase. This is what we might call design in the "waterfall" method, in which product development teams move in a linear fashion from problem to solution. While this has been the dominant design method—especially in larger corporations, as it easily creates the illusion of scientific certainty—many are starting to critique this method for holding onto a theoretical perspective for much too long. That is, teams formulate theories, present them, and finalize them, but by the time they actually act on them, it is often too late to change anything based on what they learn through enacting solutions. Teams present their vision to clients— essentially making a promise for what will be delivered—long before that vision is ever enacted in the real world. There is an admission here that the performance of theory is not necessary for the validation of that theory, which is consistent with Cartesian philosophy, but completely at odds with phenomenological design thinking.

Praxis-based design approaches—of which Lean might be one— emphasize the interaction between "internal" and "external" as the basis for design. Rapid prototyping is the primary example of a praxical design activity. The prototype is an object, but it is a disposable, fickle object used not for long-term engagement, but specifically to learn something. In this way, a prototype is more of a pseudo-object designers use to think; it is the externalization of thought into the material world in order to think beyond the head. Similar to how speech not only connects individuals but also creates its own space of truth, prototypes create connections between designers and users while also creating an emergent space independent of designer and user.

> Designing, it seems, is difficult to conduct by purely internal mental processes; the designer needs to interact with an external representation. The activity of sketching, drawing or modeling provides some of the circumstances by which a designer puts him- or herself into the design situation and engages with the exploration of both the problem and its solution. There is a cognitive limit to the amount of complexity that can be handled internally; sketching provides a temporary, external store for

tentative ideas, and supports the 'dialogue' that the designer has between problem and solution.[96]

Cross equates prototyping and sketching to interacting with problem and solution at the same time. Perhaps we might say that these activities allow an engagement with a problem space via its potential solutions. We previously showed how Donald Schön conceived of the design process as a conversation between designer and situation. Cross adds to this perspective by adding that the externalized design artifact supports that conversation, acting as a sort of materialized speech object, which serves as least two purposes: 1) to assist the designer in the act of thinking, and 2) to facilitate conversation between designers and situations, designers and users, and designers and other designers. Beyond these immediate functions, prototypes and sketches allow the exploration of potentiality.

This idea of potentiality is crucial to abductive reasoning, and therefore to design thinking. Designers must be able to consider both the present, in the form of analytical reasoning, and the future, in the form of abduction. Designers deal with the future because "technological shaping of the lifeworld happens in terms of possible technical mediations, not just actual technical mediations."[97] In the evolution of a technosocial lifeworld, it is not only the current technologies that shape our experience, but also the potential ones. Things like science fiction, research and development projects, speculative design, design fictions, and even tech advertising are phenomena that perpetuate an orientation toward potential technological scenarios—designers need to be hyper-aware of this. Within a business setting, the dualism between past and future is something Roger Martin referred to as the difference between reliability and validity.[98] Most businesses are obsessed with the quantitative data that can provide the illusion of certainty. Martin points out that quantifiable data, while highly important, will only provide insight based on what one already knows; it will not look toward the future or take potentiality into account. Reliable insights are repeatable but are not necessarily valid. Martin advocates for the intersection of valid and reliable thinking, at which point he locates design thinking.

At the root of the need to think about potentiality, Rittel and Webber shows the antinomies associated with linear movements from problems to solutions.[99] Much later, Kees Dorst refers to a design paradox. His work aims to point out the paradox of problems and solutions while exploring the prototype as a means of discovering possibilities: "Here again, the course of the problem-solving process and the very structure of the ill-structured problem are determined by the possibilities for action that the problem solver considers [...] The neat and clear design process model looses most of its value if it is preceded by a very messy and overwhelmingly influential step called 'the adoption of a prototype.'"[100] The complete understanding of a design problem is impossible before solution exploration. This is the heart of the paradox: only solutions allow us to formulate and articulate the problem space. Only through praxis-based design processes, then, can we efficiently incorporate that need to play with solutions. This idea of play and experimentation throws a sizable wrench into the waterfall design process. Prototyping forces designers to admit the fickle nature of their work; the creation of a disposable object used for thinking makes sense to designers, but often not for business-minded team members, especially clients. Designers recognize the need for situated action, but explaining that need to clients who are paying top dollar for disposable artifacts can be difficult.

Communicating that need, however, is necessary:

> Creative design seems more to be a matter of developing and refining together both the formulation of a problem and ideas for a solution, with constant iteration of analysis, synthesis, and evaluation processes between the two notional design "spaces"— problem space and solution space. In creative design, the designer is seeking to generate a matching problem-solution pair, through a coevolution of the problem and the solution. Creative design involves a period of exploration in which problem and solution spaces are evolving, and are unstable until (temporarily) fixed by an emergent bridge, which identifies a problem-solution pairing. The description of design as the coevolution of problem and solution leads to the uneasy conclusion that, in describing design, we cannot presuppose that there is something like a set "design problem" at any point in the design process.[101]

Designers need to become better at explaining the need for situated design artifacts and the fickle nature of problems and solutions. Dorst explains the latter part as problem spaces and solution spaces. If we take this metaphor literally, then surely there is no hard separation between the design space and solution space. In general, business people couldn't care less about abductive thinking and situated action, but they definitely care about risk mitigation. The merging of problem and solution spaces, praxis-based design, and an anti-dualist mindset (along with more experientially-informed approaches to design) are all means of managing risk that comes with any design project. If we are to fully eradicate the detrimental affects of dualistic design, we need to develop the language needed to articulate it. Experience designers have thus far failed to fully explore this co-existence and co-construction of problems and solutions, especially with commercial clients. The assertion itself is inherently risky and does not lend itself to project plans or budgets.

Given the nature of the problem-solution paradox, it is not something to be solved as a common problem might be. The paradox is a necessary one—an antinomy of sorts. It is only a paradox if we begin from the assumption that the movement from problem to solution is linear. But if we reframe the paradox in the light of design thinking and phenomenology, it becomes apparent that the two sides of the statement are not necessarily at odds. The solution to the problem of the paradox is more like a rethinking of the problem:

> 'Paradox' is used here in the sense of a complex statement that consists of two or more conflicting statements. In the initial state of the paradoxical problem situation, all the statements that make up the paradox are true or valid, but they cannot be combined. A paradox, a real opposition of views, standpoints, or requirements, thus requires a redefinition of the problematic situation in order to create a solution. An example from product design would be that a certain product, that cannot be moved, needs to be there to perform its function at one moment in time, and it needs to be invisible and not take up space at another moment in time. The creation of solutions to a paradoxical design situation often requires the development and creative redefinition of that situation.[102]

Our challenge is to formulate a non-dualist theory of design that reformulates our conception of design, thus rendering the paradox moot. The first step in that task might be to rethink the nature of a solution. Evgeny Morozov has done just that, referring to the tendency to think of the world as a problem to be solved as "solutionism."[103] If we can take some of Morozov's advice and realize that not every life encounter is a problem to be solved, then perhaps we can also concentrate on only the most important problems—the so-called wicked problems that require the time, attention, and money of multiple social, political, and professional organizations. But given the effects of capitalism, despite its shortcomings, this stance toward design remains mostly an ideal—experience designers in the tech industry are, for the most part, more concerned with commercial returns than with creating actual change, leading to Morozov's critique. Orienting design toward a less dualist framework is in-itself a wicked problem, involving a radical shift in the economics of who finances design, who makes money from it, and how much.

I do not claim to have the answer to this problem, or even a sufficient understanding of it. However, I believe that phenomenology can help us come to a better understanding through the articulation of a non-dualist—or at least "less dualist"—theory of design. My hope is that a new phenomenology-inspired theory of design will help overcome the solutionism and pure profit-driven design practices we see in places like Silicon Valley. That is not to say making a profit off design is a bad thing; rather, when it becomes the overwhelming norm in a certain area, the design zeitgeist begins to change in non-preferable ways. Solutionism runs rampant and we end up with isolated products designed to solve a problem that no one really has—or even worse, are both the creation and solution of a problem for profit motivation. In his theory of technological evolution, George Basalla notes the fallacy in thinking about technological objects as isolated solutions to discrete problems. In turn, he presents a theory of how technology literally evolved in the Darwinian sense to become physical manifestations of how humans choose to organize and extract meaning from their world.[104] I'm not sure I would say design solutions *never* map back to specific, discrete problems—this view seems a bit extreme. However, the normalization of solution-based design thinking certainly creates problems for design as a means of shaping the world. If designers are constantly thinking about profit-driven solutions to individual problems, they lose sight of the larger systems in which they work. Phenomenology, in its focus on holistic experience, allows designers to concentrate on how individuals experience multiple political, social, and economic systems.

To wrap up this chapter, it is worth pointing out Nelson and Stolterman's list of paradoxes in design:

1.   Design is non-attachment and total engagement.
2.   Design is flux and permanence.

3. Design is knowing and naiveté.
4. Design is experience and fresh eyes.
5. Design is collaboration and solitude.
6. Design is process and structure.
7. Design is cyclic and episodic.
8. Design is control and uncontrollable.
9. Design is unique and universal.
10. Design is infinite and finite.
11. Design is timeless and temporal.
12. Design is splendor and evil.[105]

In a certain sense, these are antinomies rather than simple paradoxes. They are not to be solved, or perhaps are not even solvable. They are contradictions that *must be*. If the state of design sways too far to one side, we end up with an ecosystem of products and services that fail to recognize design's inherent complexity. To take even one of these antinomies and define one of the poles, the results are disappointing. For example, if "design is control" were true, then we are left with a purely scientific perspective composed of controlled experiments, laboratories, and a constant regurgitation of sameness. Or if "design is naiveté" were the whole truth, designers would never get anything done. These truths need their antitheses to function. Avoiding a full descent into the Derridean rabbit hole, it is worth mentioning that these design antinomies not only need each of their poles, but also never remain static. That is, we cannot necessarily pick an optimal spot in the space between their poles, as that point is always shifting depending on the context.

What these antinomies point out is the fundamental complexity of design, which designers often attempt to push away in lieu of focusing on individual practices. Or as Bruno Latour puts it:

> Now here is the challenge: In its long history, design practice has done a marvelous job of inventing the practical skills for drawing objects, from architectural drawing, mechanic blueprints, scale models, prototyping etc. But what has always been missing from those marvelous drawings (designs in the literal sense) are an impression of the controversies and the many contradicting stake holders that are born within with these. In other words, *you* in design as well as *we* in science and technology studies may insist that objects are always assemblies, 'gatherings' in Heidegger's

meaning of the word, or things and *Dinge*, and yet, four hundred years after the invention of perspective drawing, three hundred years after projective geometry, fifty years after the development of CAD computer screens, we are still utterly unable to draw together, to simulate, to materialize, to approximate, to fully model to scale, what a thing in all of its complexity, is.[106]

Exploring this complexity is the key goal of phenomenological design thinking.

Chapter 5
Phenomenology to Post-Phenomenology to Object Studies

Critiquing Heidegger

As we have seen in the second chapter of this book, Heidegger successfully broke from the philosophy of his teacher, Edmund Husserl, and went on to develop his own unique theory of Being. His work took a massively wide-ranging approach, focusing on everything from the lofty question "what is *is?*" to language, technology, craft, poetry, and art. Philosophers following Heidegger have critiqued him on a number of points, from his use of esoteric language, to his somewhat simplistic treatment of equipment, to anti-science sentiments, to his anti-Semitism. All of these professional and personal critiques are valid. Most relevant to the current discussion, however, is his treatment of technology.

The term "post-phenomenology" has been mentioned a few times so far, but has not yet been fully defined. Don Ihde, a philosopher of technology and post-Heideggerian thinker, developed post-phenomenology as both a critique and a continuation of classical phenomenology—a critique because it calls out some of its shortcomings, particularly the treatment of technology, and a continuation because it builds on what Heidegger began, focusing on applications to newer forms of technology. Post-phenomenology differs from classical phenomenology in a few important ways:

1. Individual meaning versus essence

While Heidegger wanted to explore the essence of technology beyond any specific technological instantiations, post-phenomenology maintains that this essence, if it exists, can only be known through devices. So if we are able to know technology, we must consider individual instantiations of technology. Technology does not have a theoretical essence that plays itself out through devices, its devices shape our knowledge and understanding of it. Post-phenomenology highlights the praxical component of technology, treating individual devices as unique.

2. Industrial tech versus everyday tech

Heidegger is sometimes criticized for his failure to see outside the bounds of industrial technology. His philosophy of technology can be viewed as lacking, as its exclusive examples are things like dams and machinery specific to industry. While limiting, Heidegger's examples represent the historical context in which he was writing. They simply need to be updated, and this is exactly what post-phenomenology attempts to do, not only by choosing more modern examples but also by broadening the scope of technology. Instead of only industrial machines, we can talk about everyday objects such as pens, speed bumps, and tables as pieces of technology.

3. Technophobia to critical acceptance

Heidegger's philosophy of technology can be read as particularly technophobic, especially his views on standing reserve and the possibility for technology to put humans in a passive position (as discussed near the end of Chapter 2). These fears are certainly justified, but we must go a step further than Heidegger did. As designers, it is our responsibility to reimagine problems with technology—standing reserve being one of them—and determine what can be done. Post-phenomenology, at least implicitly, picks up where Heidegger left off and suggests that the human-technology relationship is inherently complex.

4. Mediation

The ready-to-hand relationship from Heidegger's earlier work paints a somewhat simple picture of interaction: a user acts through an object to accomplish a goal in a skillful interaction, in which the object fades to the background of the experience. What this articulation leaves out, however, is how the object acts back upon the user. Considering that the object mediates the relationship between self and world, post-phenomenology expands upon the singular human-technology interaction to show how the object acts back upon the user and actively shapes the experience.

5. New interaction styles

Post-phenomenology extends the present-at-hand and ready-to-hand to deal with the subtle nuances of interaction. As we will see in the next section, Don Ihde details four modes of interaction that account for the complexity that Heidegger either ignored or didn't recognize. We'll talk about these styles specifically in the next section.

Post-phenomenology attempts to rethink and expand Heidegger's work, and clarify certain aspects that he either did not or could not consider. For our purposes, technology is most relevant to discussions on design, as we cannot talk about technology without talking about design, and vice versa. Ihde explains the post-phenomenological position on technology as differentiated from Heidegger:

> The taking of nature as a resource well, to be challenged and its energy extracted by the technological means, reflects the notions of the late-nineteenth- and early-twentieth-century megatechnologies one usually characterizes as industrial. These were cast in terms of humans-over-nature, Promethian-style technofantasies. These are also embedded in the cultural notion that *control* is a major factor. Were technologies to be anthropological-instrumental, control might be thought to reside within the human practitioner. But, with the postwar shift, control was thought to be autonomous through the technology. Frankenstein technofantasies are simply inverted Promethian forms. Neither is the case: humans and technologies are, I argue, *interrelational* and mutually co-constitutive. Even with the pen, I 'use' the pen, but the pen with its material selectivities 'uses' me as well.[107]

Heidegger took a very a linear approach to technology and the user by assuming that humans use technology to affect nature. What he missed, however, is the idea that humans do not assert absolute control of all technological devices, as might be the case for a river dam designed to control the natural flow of water to serve some human purpose. I am reminded of Niagara Falls (where I grew up) and the amount of control the Army Corps of Engineers has over the waterfalls, which dump 150,000 gallons (American side) and 600,000 gallons (Canadian side) of water per second. The Army Corps of Engineers controls the amount of water to either increase or decrease the amount that reaches the Niagara Power Plant further down river. They can also divert the flow of water from one set of falls to the other. This is the "Promethian-style technofantasy" Ihde refers to in the quote above. This kind of control over nature is what made Heidegger so anxious.

Post-phenomenology is interested in the mundane, everyday technologies. Nevertheless, we should not confuse mundane and everyday with boring or less powerful. Our phones in our pockets might enable us to remotely control the lights in our house, transfer money to anyone in the world, or perform a multitude of tasks that would have been impossible ten years ago, but have now become mundane. While we might only experience the Promethian technologies a few times in our lives (unless one works with them), mundane technologies wrap themselves up in the minutiae of our days to introduce new ways to experience these technologies, which post-phenomenology has worked to articulate. Post-phenomenology looks for the power of technology in the minutiae of everyday life.

New Interaction Styles

Heidegger's way of thinking about interactions as present-at-hand and ready-to-hand has proven useful in design when thinking about levels of engagement users might have with a system or an object. It is certainly important for designers to be aware of the ebbs and flows between readiness and presence, and to design for systems that allow this movement without becoming disorienting. Recently, however, with the movement from a focus on large-scale industrial technology to a more modern focus on everyday devices also came the necessity to expand on Heidegger's original thoughts. Don Ihde began thinking about this need in his first book, *Technics and Praxis* published in 1979, and continued to refine his ideas in subsequent texts. He laid out four modes of interaction based on this need.

The first mode of interaction Ihde describes is embodiment relations. Similar to Heidegger's notion of the ready-to-hand relationship, embodied relations are those in which the object is fully embodied into the experience and thus fades out of focus. In a sense, the object removes itself from the equation—something else is experienced *through* the object. The example Ihde provides is a pair of eyeglasses. If someone is accustomed to wearing glasses, and given that the glasses are not smudged or broken in some way, the glasses remove themselves as an object of focus. In other words, the wearer looks *through* the glasses in order to see the world, making the main area of focus the wearer's surroundings, not the glasses. Another example from interaction design might be the touch screen. Whether on a mobile device, table, kiosk, table top, etc., the touch screen is something users act *through* in order to interact with the task at hand. Unless something gets in the way—such as when the screen is scratched or dirty—it is fully embodied into the experience.

The second mode of interaction is the hermeneutic relation. Hermeneutic relations are different from embodied relations in a few ways. First, instead of the user acting *through* the object, they act *with* the object. That is, the object is not a means of some separate experience but rather becomes a focal point of the experience itself. Second, a hermeneutic object needs to be read and interpreted to be fully experienced. It demands a bit of extra work from the user—whereas embodied objects are transparent means of accomplishment, hermeneutic objects call for our attention. A common example Peter-Paul Verbeek provides for a hermeneutic object is a thermometer. We read the thermometer to understand the world. And as a system of measurement, it is embedded in social, cultural, and linguistic norms. We experience temperature simply by existing in an environment, but the thermometer is our way of making sense of that experience. Another example might be Twitter. It is certainly a means of conversation, but it continually calls attention to itself by imposing rules such as a maximum length for each tweet or the inclusion of advertisements in a user's feed. In addition, we read the world through Twitter in a similar way as the thermometer. We experience our world from a single point, but Twitter allows us to consider multiple points of view from people around the world, thus providing the user, in some cases, with a much broader perspective on a particular topic.

It is tempting to think of embodied and hermeneutic relations as categorical—i.e., an interaction is either embodied or hermeneutic, with no overlap. Verbeek points out that the embodied and hermeneutic can be viewed as the "extreme ends of a continuum," with varying levels of mediation at each point on the line[108] (we will return to the question of mediation later in this chapter). The point here is to avoid categorizing interactions and instead think about the components of experiences that sit on the continuum between embodied and hermeneutic.

Apart from the two modes already discussed—which are probably the most obvious in terms of how they affect our conscious experience—there are two other modes Ihde describes. One is background relations, which is characterized by its lack of conscious awareness. Verbeek holds that in background relations "we are related neither explicitly to a technology nor via a technology to the world; instead, technologies shape the content of our experience in a way that is not consciously experienced."[109] He also mentions that background technologies do not play a central role in our experience. This is where things get a little muddy. While I agree on a certain level that background technologies by definition do not shape conscious experience, Verbeek's view seems unnecessarily restrictive. Experience is shaped not only by conscious awareness; it is an end result of both conscious and non-conscious environmental factors. Verbeek's example of a background technology is a refrigerator. It functions to store and preserve our food without our conscious attention, and we are certainly not usually involved with it performing this function—and yet, our lack of involvement does not equate to its lack of importance in our lives. Background technologies create the context in which embodied and hermeneutic relations can play themselves out. There is also a significant overlap between background and embodied relations. With the example of eyeglasses, it is not difficult to see how the embodied experience of wearing glasses can also be thought of as a background relation. So the difference seems less about conscious awareness, and more about proximity—not in the sense of physical proximity, but of the extent to which the technology contributes to the user's immediate experience. If we remove the glasses from someone who needs them, they will immediately notice. But if the refrigerator stops working, one might not notice until the next time they interact with it. The difference between embodied and background technologies is a question of direct involvement.

Finally, the fourth mode of experience is alterity relations, in which technology becomes quasi-other. That is, we experience alterity technologies as anthropomorphized or imbued with human-like attributes. Probably the most obvious example in modern technology is Apple's Siri—the personified virtual assistant that has been designed with a personality of "her" own. But we can also think of phrases such as "taking care of" a car or creating "intelligent machines" as indicative of the alterity relationship. Alterity seems to be the fantasy of much modern computing—from mobile devices to context-aware computing to artificial intelligence—to create a piece of technology that operates on a similar, yet importantly different level as the user.

Compared to Heidegger's conceptualization of present-at-hand and ready-to-hand relationships, we can see how Ihde has attempted to account for some of the complexity lost in Heidegger. Especially in the background and alterity relations, Ihde updates Heidegger's thinking to a more modern context, which includes an entire background of technologies and anthropomorphized devices that did not exist on the same scale in Heidegger's time. Verbeek points out that Heidegger took technology as *the* way in which worldly meaning was disclosed to Dasein, whereas Ihde concentrated on interactions with individual devices as the starting point for understanding Dasein's engagement with the world.[110] For Ihde, individual devices have different means of disclosure, and each device interaction produces a unique effect. It is not that we are engaged with the "essence of technology," which discloses its Meaning upon us; we are involved with multiple devices and use contexts, each with its own way of showing us multiple meanings. This opens the possibility to design for particular meanings, instead of a generic revealing of essence. The Heideggerian framework forces design into a sort of circular trap, relegating any sense of meaning conveyance to the strange, pseudo-transcendental "essence" of technology Heidegger holds so close. Within post-phenomenology, however, we are better equipped to think about objects as the gathering of meaning, and the extent to which that meaning is designed versus emerges.

With Ihde's interaction styles as a starting point, the remainder of this chapter on post-phenomenology will deal broadly with human interaction with designed things. As Lucy Kimbell points out, objects are of immense importance to any discourse about design;[111] after all, objects are often the end result of a design process, even in the case of experience design or service design, in which tangibility is less emphasized but networks of objects might be a result. Until recently, however, design theory has largely ignored objects as serious focal points for study. Movements such as post-phenomenology, object-oriented ontology, actor-network theory, and the aptly named "thing theory" have all made efforts to highlight objects as a primary focus. While all these fields have touched on design, however, it is not of central importance. We will return later to how these theories can contribute to a larger phenomenological design theory. A quick note on the nature of things is helpful here before returning to the topic in chapter 7.

Even with Heidegger's obsession with "essence," we can also see an emphasis on individual things as the means of enacting being: "[Dasein] finds *itself* primarily and constantly *in things* because, tending them, distressed by them, it always in some way or other rests in things. Each one of us is what he pursues and cares for. In everyday terms, we understand ourselves and our existence by way of the activities we pursue and the things we take care of."[112] Self-understanding, for Heidegger, is a result of the actions we take in the world and the objects we use to complete those actions. Not surprisingly, Heidegger does not accept that a concept of the self can be divorced from its context. Understanding the self is always contingent on interaction with something—we need to extend ourselves beyond the limits of an isolated mind, become involved with things, and experience the self through the medium of objects.

Post-phenomenological thinking often deals with reciprocation, where one movement has a countermovement. For example, mediation acts to sit in the middle of an interaction and connect poles of experience (as we touched on briefly in the previous section). Thus, when we say that interacting with objects provides the user a sense of self-understanding—that one is only able to act and know through the lens of objects—the same is true for objects: they obtain an identity via human interaction. For example, a desk is only a desk in relation to what we do with it. Put dinner plates on a desk and it becomes a dining table. Put religious artifacts on a desk and it becomes part of a shrine. The word "desk" is arbitrary, as nothing about the word "desk" points to what we know as "desk-ness."[113] It is only what we do with the desk that designates it as such. Or, in post-phenomenological terms:

> 'The' world does not exist for us; we can only access 'our' world, which is the world as it is disclosed *by us*. From this perspective, it is impossible to speak about technology without taking into account the relationship people have with it. An artifact without people relating to it would be no more than a 'piece of junk lying around.' It becomes a technology only *in relation to people*. A technology is always a technology-to..., and this 'to-...' gives the artifact its identity.[114]

The interaction goes both ways: the objects gives the user identity, and the user gives the object identity. This relationship is at the heart of Samuel Beckett's novel *Malone Dies*, mentioned earlier. Malone relies on his objects—sticks, pencils, pots, carts—to give his life meaning as he sits on his bed in a dark room. They are literally his entire world. And, at the same time, his objects gain identity through interaction—a stick with a hooked end becomes an extension of Malone's arm when attempting to reach other objects across the room. The pencil is his way of thinking

This dual relationship between objects and users is of massive importance to design, but is often left out of the conversation regarding end results of design objects. We release objects into the world not only to serve the planned, destined, desired outcomes that designers and their clients are both complicit in fetishizing; these objects also have a powerful tendency to create emergent meaning from their interaction with other entities in a system. As we will see in the following sections, this idea that objects assume an active role in the human-world relationship—and thus the results of design cannot be planned with certainty—is at the heart of phenomenological design thinking. And, it is a major point that post-phenomenology espouses—that there is an intimate, complex relationship between body and world to the point that the understanding of one is completely dependent on the other:

> [W]e grasp the unity of our body only in that of the thing, and it is by taking things as our starting point that our hands, eyes and all our sense-organs appear to us as so many interchangeable instruments. The body by itself, the body at rest is merely an obscure mass, and we perceive it as a precise and identifiable being when it moves toward a thing, and in so far as it is intentionally projected outwards, and even then this perception is never more than incidental and marginal to consciousness, the centre of which is occupied with things and the world.[115]

The relationship between body, thing, and world will be a common theme as we begin to understand the necessity of seemingly "external" things in the world. This is what Ihde attempts to give us with his interaction styles: means of reading our interactions with things, which is essentially making sense of how we make sense.

Mediation and the Human-Technology Relationship

Don Ihde's interaction styles are unique because they assume that each device is unique in how it participates in the generation of meaning; they avoid the assumption that devices and objects are simply tools that humans use to accomplish goals. While the instrumental view of technology is true—as Heidegger would certainly argue—it is only partially true. As post-phenomenologists and actor-network theorists have argued, objects are not neutral aspects of the environment—they are active participants in human-environment systems. The current section will focus on how technology mediates our experience of the world, with the end goal of articulating how understanding the active nature of objects can result in more well-rounded designers.

It is very natural for designers to talk about their work as a result of societal influences, user needs, desires, and pains. For example, the popular house-sharing platform Airbnb is said to have been born out of the need for more affordable or unique lodging options, along with the availability of extra space. In other words, there are people with available houses, apartments, rooms, and couches who are willing to rent them to travelers looking for either a cheap place to stay or simply a more "authentic" feel than a hotel room can provide. These two forces resulted in Airbnb, a platform that allows for exactly that. From this angle, societal (capitalist) forces result in a design solution that results in higher convenience often at a lower price. However, from a different angle, we can see a very different interpretation. It is necessary for Airbnb to provide its customers with a certain amount of security, akin to what they would receive at a hotel or traditional bed and breakfast. At a hotel, one makes a reservation and feels relatively sure they will have a room upon arrival, as hotels, especially chains, attempt to instill a sense of reliability and security to its guests. With Airbnb, one is renting from an individual, so in order to provide the same sense of reliability, they encourage user reviews. Each person who provides or rents space has a profile, which includes reviews from previous stays. The space provider will rate their renter on how well they communicate, whether they were loud or disrespectful, cleanliness, etc. Similarly, the renter will rate the space based on cleanliness, trueness to photos as advertised, neighborhood, etc. One might argue that these types of interactions result in a commodification of trust, and can create a sense of competition between individuals (instead of between businesses, in the case of hotels). Airbnb is often touted as an example of the democratization of lodging in that it provides consumers with choice, but there is a cost involved when we begin to see our neighbors as competitors and how the service should be regulated.

Regardless of one's view on Airbnb and similar "sharing economy" products, the example shows how, from one point of view, the product is a result of societal factors, and from another angle, it creates new societal factors that did not exist—at least not at scale, previously. "Societies are not only held together by social relations and institutions, as sociologists and anthropologists claim, but by things as well. Technology should be analysed not only in terms of the social processes in which it is constructed, but also in terms of the role it plays in social processes itself."[116] We might say that there is a reciprocal relationship between social relations and objects: relations result in objects, which results in new relations, and so on. The important part is to recognize the extent to which objects function to act back upon the society and the individuals who create them. Especially when designing objects and experiences, recognition of their active role is a crucial, ethical responsibility. In general, Airbnb users will not critically analyze their use of the service (they will simply use it), but it will shape their behavior, likely in ways they will never notice. "Being a designer" involves a sense of foresight into the preferred way of being in the world. It is the designer's job to assume this critical role and actively shape the conditions of experience. Designers are special because they take care to articulate that vision and attempt to craft it.

These examples allude to Peter-Paul Verbeek's conception of mediation, which begins with the assertion that "[t]echnologies coshape the human world and thus also human relations with technology itself. Human beings are not sovereign with respect to technology, but are, rather, inextricably interwoven with it" and that mediation is the force that "shapes the mutual relation in which both subject and object are concretely constituted. Someone who wears eyeglasses, for instance, is not the same without them."[117] Technology is both part of the human and of the environment. It can be a fully embodied pair of eyeglasses of which the wearer is completely unconscious. It can also be a pair of eyeglasses the wearer removes and places on the table, at which point it becomes an object in the environment, with all the hermeneutic implications that come with it. If you are sensing a bit of a contradiction here, it is because mediation comes very close to undermining the theoretical foundations on which it is built—specifically, that Dasein accounts for an "undifferentiated" world in which subject and object are simply related forces in the same system. Verbeek falls back on the vocabulary of "subject" and "object," seemingly to illustrate how the two forces are balanced in the act of mediation—i.e., there is no hierarchy of subject acting upon object.

We are currently seeing an entire ecosystem of products and services that illustrate the ability for technology to act back upon its users. The Internet of Things is a system of internet-connected, or "smart," objects, from everyday things like toasters and thermostats to industrial equipment used on farms. I have no idea what shape the Internet of Things will take, or if it will even exist at all (by the time this book is published), but it is worth pointing out the premises on which it is built and how they relate to mediation. At its core, the Internet of Things movement attempts to create objects that assume a certain amount of agency. For example, the Nest thermostat allows users to regulate temperatures from anywhere in the world, and beyond that, Nest will learn patterns of behavior and adjust accordingly in order to save energy and money. Nest assumes a certain amount of autonomy, allowing it to move fluidly between hermeneutic relations when a user checks and adjusts the temperature, to background relations when it actively shapes the environment through automation. The Internet of Things is an extreme example of technology shaping the environment, but certainly we can speak of everyday objects such as furniture, clothing, and other "dumb" things as active agents in the world.

To really understand the nature of mediation, it is necessary to spend some time on the idea of context and how it affects our experience of the world. The word "context," when broken into its parts, simply means "with text." Following post-structuralist lines of thought, we can think of a text as something to be interpreted, and that can result in a multiplicity of meanings.[118] In this sense, context consists of the peripheral information we use to interpret any given situation. Within design, performing qualitative user research is a great example of the importance of context—not simply the importance performing research in the context of use, but also the idea that the object of research cannot be determined directly, instead necessitating an exploration of the periphery. For example, if we want to determine levels of satisfaction among people who rent spare rooms on Airbnb, one approach might be to simply ask them. While direct, this strategy runs the risk of introducing significant bias into the study. When simply asked, participants will be influenced by a number of biases, including the desire to please others when in conversation, selective memory (whether good or bad), etc. Perhaps a better way to frame this type of research is to ask about the last few times they hosted a guest, what their overall experience was like, and what drove them to rent a room on Airbnb, allowing experiential factors to emerge on their own. This latter technique is certainly more broad and requires a much more involved interpretation process; but by probing the context, results will be much more reliable and less influenced by bias.

The idea here is that context shapes experience. For example, while interacting with our phones is interesting, considering that interaction in context is what is truly compelling. The periphery shapes the experience. Even using the same product across contexts is completely different—the experience with Facebook is different if the user is at home on the couch, versus in a security line at the airport, versus at their desk at work. Both context and mediation force designers to think at the level of systems: "The pile of matter that we call an 'automobile' can only exist as such in a context that includes also gasoline, pumps, refineries, highways, auto mechanics, automobile manufacturing plants, and so forth. What exists 'in itself' is only metal and synthetic material."[119] Only materials that exist with larger systems of relations are meaningful, as the act of mediation is inseparable from meaning generation. This is because mediation is a constitutive act, rather than a simple interplay between subject and object: "Mediating technologies are no 'inter-mediaries' that 'convey' specific aspects of the objective world to the minds of subjects; they are mediators that help to constitute what is real for us, and what we are in relation to that reality"[120]

Mediation constitutes our world in conjunction with the unpredictability of object use and the agency of things. To illustrate this point, it is helpful to consider a bit of a polemical example: the gun. Many thinkers from post-phenomenology and actor-network theory have considered this example. On one hand, a gun is something one picks up and uses for very specific purposes—target practice, sport hunting, committing murder, etc. The gun has become a symbol of things like gang violence, police control, and murder in the United States. The National Rifle Association, an organization committed to protecting the right to bear arms, has attempted to battle against the negative view of guns by adopting the slogan "guns don't kill people…people kill people." The message, of course, is that we should not blame guns for gun violence; the responsibility lies with the human who pulls the trigger. The human is the active agent who decides to commit the act, and the gun is simply one of many instruments that can accomplish the end goal. Murder is murder, whether committed with a gun, knife, rock, poison, etc. While undoubtedly a pithy and hard-hitting slogan that has convinced many people that gun control might not be the answer to the problem of gun violence, a view inspired by post-phenomenology and actor-network theory would question the core premise. While the person with the gun might be legally responsible for the act, the slogan ignores the idea that holding a gun literally changes someone. Someone with a gun is certainly very different than someone without a gun, which is why we call the former a "gunman." The introduction of a gun creates a new hybrid entity, showing how the gun mediates the situation to create reality. The simple act of holding a gun combines object and user into a "gunman," which is different from either entity by itself.

Pushing the example a bit further, we can see how context can also drastically change situations involving guns. Consider the following people in their particular situations: police officer on duty, masked man in a bank, soldier in combat, child at home, hunter in the woods, and a teen at school. Some of these fit the context quite well, while others certainly do not. A police officer on duty carrying a gun is no surprise, but a man at a bank has no business with a weapon unless he is planning a robbery. Even further than their roles and environments, mindset plays heavily into the interaction. Is the police officer pointing his gun at the man in the bank or at the teen in school? Or at an innocent third party? Each variation results in a vastly different role for the human-gun relationship, all with their own ethical considerations.

Of course, the gun is a very extreme example, especially within the context of design. However, it illustrates a few points we have covered in this section and the previous one: 1) Technology mediates the relationship between self and world; 2) Mediation is not simply an intermediary between two opposing poles, but it also helps constitute the entire experience; 3) The movement between interaction styles can be quite fluid. Design comes into play when thinking about the importance of context—not simply from a research-in-context perspective, but also from the sense that the outcomes of a design process, whether tangible or intangible, will be used in highly contextual situations. Context, as it were, goes both ways: we must understand it prior to the generation of solutions, but of equal importance, we must attempt to gather foresight into how design solutions will affect the contextual situations in which they exist. This latter point is immensely difficult, but as designers, this is our job—to take advantage of abductive thinking and concentrate on what *could be*.

This short examination of context shows the importance of context and the importance/difficulty of designing for mediation. If mediation works to create the experience and is a crucial part of human interaction with any object, how are designers to create desired mediations? The answer to this question is certainly not a simple one. A place to start would be looking at the specificity of things in context. In the examples above of different people in different situations, all holding a gun, we can see how replacing the gun with a knife or any other weapon without the cultural and societal implications of a firearm will change the situation. Similarly, in design, the meaning of an object coupled with its function is what mediates the experience: "People can only develop a durable relationship with artifacts if what matters is not just a matter of style or function. After all, other artifacts could embody the same meaningfulness or functionality, but no other artifact can be this specific material thing, here and now."[121] Function and situated meaning, "here and now," are the fuel of mediation.

As we will see in the next chapter, similar to how we might assume humans act upon objects intentionally, we sometimes also assume designers act upon problem spaces linearly to conclude in solutions. Much recent design theory would not agree, advocating instead for a more reciprocal relationship between the designer and the space of design. Perhaps most famously, Donald Schön explained the design process as a conversation:

> According to Schön, designing proceeds as 'a reflective conversation with the situation,' an interactive process based on posing a problem frame and exploring its implications in 'moves' that investigate the arising solution possibilities. A designer, he argued, is faced with a situation of complexity. 'Because of this complexity, the designer's moves tend, happily or unhappily, to produce consequences other than those intended. When this happens, the designer may take account of the unintended changes he has made in the situation by forming new appreciations and understandings and by making new moves. He shapes the situation, in accordance with his initial appreciation of it, the situation "talks back", and he responds to the situation's back-talk.'[122]

We might say that the designer speaks intention into the design space, and the design space actively communicates back what will work and what might not, hinting to possible outcomes of introducing a new object or experience into a system. In the next two sections, we will look deeper at the notion of designer intention and the unpredictability of designed objects and experiences.

Intentionality

I don't believe it's a stretch to say most designers would like to believe they are actively influencing a system outside themselves. However, most designers can make the distinction between influencing and dictating, and it would likely be difficult to find a designer who believes they have the ability to elicit specific effects on a system with any kind of reliability or certainty. Instead, designers create the conditions of possibility for desired outcomes, but this in no way guarantees or even suggests that these outcomes will come to fruition. Design history is full of examples of creative misuse, or how users co-opt technological objects for purposes other than what was intended. We will see some examples of creative misuse later in this section. For now, we should point out that having a strong design intention is not detrimental—rather, it is just necessary to know the limits of intentionality and not get caught up in the linear trap of thinking design moves from problem to solution. Having strong, clearly articulated intent helps to balance the effects of mediation as a constitutive force.

In his work on actor-network theory (ANT), Bruno Latour asks, "What is a tool?"[123] ANT attempts to formulate a theory of human-object interaction in which humans are not always the active agent who acts upon the object. Latour and others called for a reformulation of the very word "agent" into the more specific "actant," to refer to anything, living or non-living, that imposes intention within a system. This conception leaves room for both human and non-human actants. Thus, his answer to the question "What is a tool?" is: "The extension of social skills to nonhumans." I believe we can take the word "extension" to mean not simply a teaching or a passing-down, but rather a recognition. In this case, the recognition is in that objects have the power to change systems, that they are not simply dead material used for attaining goals, as we have seen with the gun example. Thus, by extending social skills to object, we are recognizing their ability to mediate, speak, and manipulate in the same way human actants do.

Design influences how we extend sociality. Social skills are not innate; they must be taught and absorbed through the lens of culture. Design helps to determine the aspects of sociality appropriate for an object or experience, and attempts to inscribe them into its creation. However, it is problematic to directly link design intention with this inscription. In this sense, we cannot design without intent, and this intention becomes embedded into objects: "Each artifact has its script, its 'affordance,' its potential to take hold of passersby and force them to play roles in its story."[124] Despite Latour's strange use of the word "affordance" (which we will cover in the next chapter), his point about objects wrapping-up others in a story is key. As we saw with the gun-related scenarios, actants play various roles: the police officer as that of enforcer, the child at school as that of chaos creator, the gun as that of instrument of violence, and an almost infinite number of other roles. But of equal importance for design is the recognition that the things we design take on new meanings after they are released into the world. Intention does not, by any means, account for the entirety of design. There are other forces beyond the designer's control that have equal influence on design.

One example of how designer intention plays itself out is through scripts. For Latour, scripts are how objects enact their sociality in the world. They are inscribed purposes that allow objects to assume in the engagement with other actants and entities in a system, specifically designed for certain purposes:

> According to Latour, scripts are often, though not always, the products of 'inscriptions' by designers. Designers anticipate how users will interact with the product they are designing and, implicitly or explicitly, build prescriptions for use into the materiality of the product. Latour describes this inscription process in terms of 'delegation': designers delegate specific responsibilities to artifacts. To a speed bump, for instance, the responsibility was delegated to make sure nobody drives too fast.[125]

Verbeek mentions one of Latour's favorite examples of a script: speed bumps. If designers are working toward the end goal of slowing traffic, they have a few options for meeting that goal: 1) They can put up a sign that says "slow down" to encourage drivers to hit the breaks; 2) They can install a radar display that shows drivers how fast they are going, and how it compares to the speed limit; 3) They can redesign the road with sharp curves so drivers have no choice but to go slow; 4) They can install speed bumps. The list can go on. With the first option, drivers must rely on their own sense of morality and responsibility, and many will find it very easy to simply ignore the sign, either on purpose or by just not applying too much thought. The second option works to make the driver hyper-aware of his or her speed, thus instilling responsibility on a conscious level to hopefully, then, influence behavior. The third and especially the fourth options offload the moral responsibility of the driver onto the object. The driver does not choose to slow down, they *must* slow down in order to avoid veering off the road or causing damage to their vehicle. Designers, in this case, have chosen to instill the objects with the power to not only influence human action but to (almost) dictate it.

Another famous example deals with keys at hotels. While most hotels have replaced keys with electronic cards that can be swiped at the door, Latour tells a story of a hotel manager who used physical keys for guests, who would then run into the problem of losing the keys when they left for the day. Guests would return without the key, and the manager would have to pay to get replacements made. Faced with a financial problem, he decided to put up a sign at the lobby door asking guests to drop off their keys at the front desk before leaving. Of course, it is very easy to ignore a sign, so the manager began asking guests to leave their keys when exiting the hotel. Realizing that he cannot catch every single guest walking out the door, and how annoying it must be to constantly be badgered, he came up with another solution. He attached large, cumbersome keychains to each key. The keychains held big pieces of wood that would be impossible or at least highly impractical to place in a pants pocket or even a backpack. The piece of wood asked guests to leave the key at the front desk. Similarly to the speed bump example, the final solution removes the burden of choice from the user, and instills the object with decision-making power.

In each of these examples, designers made conscious decisions to ostensibly decrease the burden of choice for the user. From the beginning of the industry we know as user experience design, we have heard the mantra of "don't make me think," or the rhetoric of making each action as mindless as possible. While this works well with more transactional interactions, there are times when stripping the agency from the human actant can be quite jarring. Latour explains the case of the automatic seat belt:

Early this morning, I was in a bad mood and decided to break a law and start my car without buckling my seat belt. My car usually does not want to start before I buckle the belt. It first flashes a red light 'FASTEN YOUR SEAT BELT!,' then an alarm sounds; it is so high pitched, so relentless, so repetitive, that I cannot stand it. After ten seconds I swear and put on the belt. This time, I stood the alarm for twenty seconds and then gave in. My mood had worsened quite a bit, but I was at peace with the law—at least with that law. I wished to break it, but I could not. Where is the morality? In me, a human driver, dominated by the mindless power of an artifact? Or in the artifact forcing me, a mindless human, to obey the law that I freely accepted when I get my driver's license? Of course, I could have put on my seat belt before the light flashed and the alarm sounded, incorporating in my own self the good behavior that everyone— the car, the law, the police—expected of me. Or else, some devious engineer could have linked the engine ignition to an electric sensor in the seat belt, so that I could not even have started the car before having put it on. Where would the morality be in those two extreme cases? In the electric currents flowing in the machine between the switch and the sensor? Or in the electric currents flowing down my spine in the automatism of my routinized behavior?[126]

It is easy for designers to forget the massive implications their decisions make. The current state of experience design, especially in the United States, is becoming worrisome for this reason. Startup culture fueled by venture capitalist motives, the fetishization of documentation, focus on profit and speed, and new methodologies aimed at continuous learning but so easily bastardized into a hyper-design and speed-driven technique are contributing to the erosion of reflection and contemplation in experience design. Experience designers work with mostly intangible design solutions (experiences), and I'm not convinced we have taken the time to understand the implications of *designing an experience*. I hope this book will make a small contribution to that project in setting up some key questions around how to design experiences that meet design goals, but also maintain some sort of equilibrium between human and non-human actants. Much of this effort depends on how we talk about the problem. As Heidegger states, "It is language that tells us about the nature of a thing, provided that we respect language's own nature. In the meantime, to be sure, there rages round the earth an unbridled yet clever talking, writing and broadcasting of spoken words. Man acts as though *he* were the shaper and master of language, while in fact *language* remains the master of man."[127]

Designer intent has always been a problematic topic in the experience design world. Some experience designers have latched on to the idea that "design is the rendering of intent"[128] as a grounding for understanding their work. While this definition is true, it is also overly simplistic and misleading. All design involves intent, but the role intent plays is much more complex than any pithy statement. It's like saying the sky is blue: of course it is true, but it doesn't deal with the complexity of the situation. Sometimes the sky is different colors; it is black at night, orange at sunset, grey when overcast with clouds. So while design in general is the materialization of a designer's intent, as we saw in the previous examples of scripts, this only accounts for a very small part of design under the guise of explaining any and all design, and is therefore of little use. The main problem, I believe, is how we talk about intent. It is easy to discuss the role of intent in design and conclude that if the designer wants a certain outcome, they will design the means by which those outcomes occur. And while this view is completely valid, it ignores everything that happens after the design solution is created—namely, its success according to the original goals and any user-driven interactions that were not part of the designer's intention. So intent is important, but we must also consider its limitations.

Intent is more than simply wanting something to happen and taking steps to encourage a certain outcome. The word "intent" has roots in a few languages, mostly Latin, where it can be taken literally to mean "stretch out," "lean toward," or "strain." The verb form "intend" literally means "to stretch toward" or "to direct one's attention to." We get the sense that intention deals with orienting oneself toward a future object or future state—leaning towards it, stretching out to reach it, and directing all attention toward it. It is not difficult to see how the entire design process can be seen as the practice of intention; a designer examines a problem space, comes to a solution, and takes steps to map out the specific means of making his or her intention materialize in the world. Within this process, designers experience many of the phenomena discussed in chapter 3: the idea that forethought guides the design process—where designers are so constantly oriented toward a future state that they use abductive thinking to imagine *what could be* according to their intention—and that throughout the entire process they are orienting themselves completely toward the design solution. But again, this view only describes the process of design itself and ignores everything afterwards. I believe that a rich design theory needs to consider not only the design process itself but also the effects of design.

Wimsatt and Beardsley reimagined much of literary criticism when they put forth their theory of the intentional fallacy.[129] The intentional fallacy holds that judging a text based on assumed authorial intent is a mistake. Of course, every author has an intent when producing a text—a desired outcome or feeling they want to instill in the reader. Wimsatt and Beardsley argue that this intent is completely unknowable; even if the critic asks the author "what was your intent?" the answer is moot. They argue that the text stands on its own and should be interpreted without the author's influence. The text exists independently of its creator and, in a sort of Latourian sense, exerts its own influence on the world. This of course paved the way for post-structuralist thinkers who argued that the author is simply a function of the text, and once the text is released into the world, the author no longer matters when considering the value of the text.[130] Our question is whether this view applies to design.

There are plenty of differences between a text and a design solution, the most pressing of which is the question of constraints. For a true text, which opens up the possibilities for multiple interpretations, the constraints are minimal or non-existent.[131] Design, however, is often defined by its need to mediate multiple, often conflicting, constraints. For this reason, I would argue that the intention of the designer is still relevant when judging the value of design, as the criteria for this judgment are, at least in part, determined by how well they addressed the problem while navigating constraints. Don Ihde explored the notion of intentional fallacy in design and named a similar phenomenon: the designer fallacy. He critiqued the reliance on intent by stating:

> [T]he designer fallacy is 'deistic' in its 18th century sense, that the designer-god, working with plastic material, creates a machine or artifact which seems 'intelligent' by design – and performs in its designed way. Instead, I hold, the design process operates in very different ways, ways which imply a much more complex set of inter-relations between any designer, the materials which make the technology possible, and the uses to which any technologies may be put.[132]

Being a philosopher of technology as opposed to a design theorist, Ihde's focus is on the outcomes of design rather than design itself. He calls into question the implicit notion of the designer-god deity (*de*-sign) who creates a solution according to desired functions, and those functions are played out in the world. Ihde argues that design solutions offer a multitude of alternate uses far beyond any original intention. By itself, this point is quite obvious; but considered within the overall context of design theory, it represents an important consideration for the effects of design.

In chapter 4, we touched on Donald Schön's idea that design is a conversation between designer and situation. Designer intention allows us to push the metaphor a bit further. '
"Conversation" is a good choice of words here, as it implies a reciprocal interaction—a mediation of intention and reality. In this way, the design "conversation" is an emergent effect of the design process itself, in which intention is only one of many influencing factors: "We say that we "conduct" a conversation, but the more genuine a conversation is, the less its conduct lies within the will of either partner. Thus a genuine conversation is never the one that we wanted to conduct."[133] So while we like to believe designer intention plays into the design process and creates the means of interaction to accomplish intended goals, the end use of design solutions is more of an emergent phenomenon that reveals itself through human interaction. The designer creates the conditions of possibility for certain outcomes, but the actual outcomes lie outside both the designer and the user. They exist in a system of entities including designers, users, and object/experience.

Classical phenomenology, mostly from Heidegger and Husserl's work, talks about intentionality a bit differently than we have so far. Husserl says that we are intentional beings—that is, our consciousness is always consciousness *of something*. We are never simply conscious in a general sense.

> Rather than separating humans and world, the concept of intentionality makes visible the inextricable connections between them. Because of the intentional structure of human experience, human beings can never be understood in isolation from the reality in which they live. Humans are always directed toward reality. They cannot simply 'think,' but they always think something; they cannot simply 'see,' but they always see something; they cannot simply 'feel' but always feel something.[134]

So our consciousness is always grounded in the things around us; any action is directed at an object, thus linking the object and human into a system of interactions. From the other side, if we think about the intentionality of objects, we need to acknowledge the difference between the natural world and the built world. Maarten Franssen explains the difference in the following passage, which is worth quoting in its entirety:

> [T]echnical artifacts are created with a purpose in mind that transcends the designer's act of creation, a purpose that clings to the artifact, so to speak, after its creator has left the stage. This is indeed how we conceptualize technical artifacts in everyday life: our toolbox is filled with objects that we think of as being screwdrivers, wrenches, and so forth. The 'for-ness' clinging to technical artifacts eludes the physical description of nature. [...] A bottle that I use temporarily as the support for a stick at the top of which I am fastening something, changes from being for containing liquids to being for holding a stick upright and then back again to being for containing liquids. If we think of an artifact as something that definitely is for something, as a defining property, this seems unacceptable. However, we do accept it in the case of natural objects that we use for a purpose. This stone was not for anything, it is now for cracking a nut, and it will again be not for anything in a few minutes time. I may want to crack another nut in a moment, but I can pick up any other available stone for this, in complete disregard of the first stone's ephemeral existence as a nut- cracker. Similarly I could pick another bottle for the next stick. Indeed, as far as the purpose of holding a stick upright is concerned, it does not matter whether the bottles are artifacts and in that sense already 'for something'. They are chosen because they have the right physical properties, just as the stones have the right physical properties for the job of cracking a nut. If bottles grew on trees, that would be just as fine: and indeed, in some countries bottles, i.e., things having the right properties for containing liquids and for keeping sticks upright, do grow on trees. How much do we gain by claiming that bottles – our bottles, made of glass or plastic – essentially are for containing liquids and that gourds essentially are natural objects that, accidentally, can be used for containing liquids?[135]

The big difference between what Franssen calls technical artifacts and a natural object is, generally speaking, its *for-ness*. As we saw in earlier discussions, a designed object is designed *for something*, similarly to how consciousness is consciousness *of something*. Artifacts have scripts that designers have built, which "cling to the object" long after the designer has left. Natural tools like rocks and sticks ostensibly have no scripts or intended actions associated with them, as they were not designed. But as Franssen shows, the distinction between natural and artificial is blurred when we consider how people use these objects. This is because natural objects have physical properties that communicate potential use (we will discuss this further in the next chapter with the theory of affordances). There is a certain plasticity in natural objects, as anyone who has used a stone to prop open a door can attest. And even with designed artifacts, we can see how some are designed specifically to mask their designer's intentions, or at least to open up the possibilities of use. One example is Twitter, which is essentially an open communication platform in which users craft their own experience according to who they choose to follow and which conversations they entertain. Another perhaps more extreme example is Second Life: a virtual world in which users can design their own second virtual life. It began as a relatively confined virtual landscape, and has since been built up to a vast area of digital geography. The potential for interaction is almost limitless, and there are almost no pre-determined paths one must follow. The intention built into these products is precisely to undermine the very idea of designer intention.

Creative misuse is the phenomenon of users breaking the intended use cases designers have set out to encourage. Some of the most interesting parts of the design process come when considering how users adapt a product to their needs. Examples of creative misuse can be as mundane as using a hammer as a paper weight. Of course, the script or intended action for a hammer is to pound a nail. But when in a situation that calls for a heavy object to weigh down a stack of papers, and no other more suitable option is available, one can easily adapt the function of a hammer to fit the immediate needs. Other examples of creative misuse include using the side of a table to remove a beer bottle cap, or placing a tie on a doorknob to keep others out of the room. The latter example is my personal favorite, not only because it's a little scandalous, but also because it shows how people will creatively solve their own problems. In this case, the tie on the doorknob means "this door doesn't have a lock or multiple people have a key, and don't come in because people are having sex in here." The tie seems to communicate a cultural memory to those who can "read" it. While certainly not its intended function, the tie says "do not disturb," thus undermining its function as neckwear. Even as I write this paragraph aboard a plane, the man across the aisle has discovered that his entertainment system, which is propped up from the side of his chair by an arm, is broken and cannot support the screen. He is attempting to prop it up by tying rubber bands he obtained from a flight attendant and by stuffing napkins in the various joints on the support arm. None of these are working very well for him, but it serves as a serendipitous and timely example of creatively misusing tools, napkins, and rubber bands (in this case) to solve for broken things or bad design.

While designer intention is important, it is not by any means the only, or even the most important, driving force in design. But intention is not completely irrelevant within the design process either, as some critics have argued in literary theory. What creative misuse shows us is that "agents who typically use artifacts can occasionally, or even regularly, be designers, i.e., the constructors and communicators of use plans."[136] While the sentiment is correct, I disagree with the idea that anyone using artifacts is a designer. I believe that everyone designs and participates in the activity of changing their environment, but that does not make everyone a designer. As we saw in chapter 3, the designer identity is shaped by a particular care and concern for design, an orientation of Dasein toward the mindset and thinking of design. Nevertheless, it seems to be part of human nature to contrive our environment according to certain purposes. Creative misuse allows designers to think about these contrivances and gain insight into the un-discovered needs, wants, and desires of end users.

Many of the discussions in this section and the previous one are contingent on one of the most important post-phenomenological concepts: multistability. Mediation, decreased influence of designer intention, and creative misuse are all results of multistable technology. In the next section, we'll focus on what multistability is and how it affects the design process.

Multistability

Throughout this chapter, I have alluded to an affect that drives mediation and makes simple intention cause-and-effect statements problematic. It is an effect that makes design exciting; that makes designers think beyond the object or experience they are designing. It holds that technology is not pure instrumentality—that is, technological objects have scripts and intentions behind them, but their actual use is something Don Ihde calls multistable. Multistability accounts for the difference between what designers want to occur and what actually occurs. It holds that technology takes shape not according to what it is but rather what it can do. Previously we saw how post-phenomenology expands on Heidegger's view of technology to include possibilities that were not yet considered—multistability is how we can account for those effects.

Multistability holds that technology literally has multiple stabilities within its relationship to humans. The scripts designers embed are only a portion of potential roles the design solutions can assume in any interactive system. The mode of mediation is multistable in its ability to shift its role at various times. In its simplest form, technology can mean different things at different times, to different users with different needs. It is important to note that Ihde did not designate technology as "unstable." The technological system is not completely without stability or stable meaning—as designed scripts do assert some influence—but that influence varies by context. Thus, multistability shows how technologies can be interpreted, used, and experienced differently across situations. In one context, a mobile phone is a device for accessing email when not at a desk in front of a computer. In another context, it might serve a very different purpose of an imaginary point of focus when trying to avoid eye contact with someone in the room. Each situation is a point of stability from which we can understand the technological device within the larger system of interactions that it exists.

Multistability is the characteristic of technology that helps round out our discussions of mediation and intentionality. If technologies were not multistable—that is, if they performed exactly according to scripts designers intend, and do not affect the larger system of actors and interactions in which they exist—then we would have no reason to consider mediation and the fickle nature of designer intention. If experience designers are true to their title, they should be very much concerned with systems of use for the things they design. If we spend all our time focused only on profit-driven projects that aim to scale design down to its most atomistic parts, then we end up designing things like Airbnb, which, despite its convenience and popularity, results in some questionable effects on everyday life. Instead, if experience designers are literally *designing experiences* and not simply designing screens, then we have to determine a more rigorous approach to thinking about human-technology systems, including how to educate our clients on its value.

I don't claim to have any hard answers to this problem, but I think post-phenomenology can give us a good place to start by challenging some of the assumptions experience designers often make about the world. In the United States at least, many designers are excellent craftspeople but often lack the systems approach to designing experiences. They can design screens all day, and do it quite well, but thinking about future scenarios for their products or thinking through how the product fits within a larger service system is a completely different story. However, the notion of context and the variability of situational influences is familiar to even the most hyper-focused craftsperson, so that statements such as the following are not conceptually foreign: "[T]he mediating capacity of artifacts is no essential property of things themselves, but emerges from the interplay of things and their context. Technologies are 'multistable', as Ihde observes, in that they are what they are only within the context in which they are used. What things are, and therefore how they mediate the mutual constitution of people and the world, emerges from people's relationships with them."[137] Specifically that powerful phrase "they are what they are only within the context in which they are used," while possibly a bit too all-or-nothing for some craftspeople, is still a familiar concept. That is to say, designers and craftspeople of all kinds seem particularly aware of context, so even the most hyper-focused craftspeople seem capable of thinking in systems—they might simply need a good framework. There is some activity in this space with methods such has service design and systemic design. The evolution of these frameworks will certainly contribute to a more robust experience design approach.

So the designer side of the equation is in a good, albeit preliminary place. The other side, however—the client side that often finances design projects in the hopes of turning a profit—seems particularly invested in not thinking at a system level, as it adds a certain amount of complexity and uncertainty. Commercial clients, as a whole, seem to have trouble with concepts such as the radical variability of technological objects: "Technologies do not determine directions in any hard sense. [...] [W]hile humans using technologies enter into interactive situations whenever they use even the simplest technology—and thus humans use and are used by that technology, and all such relations are interactive—the possible uses are always ambiguous and multistable."[138] Ambiguity is a necessary evil within design. Clients prefer to not think about the design solutions they finance as having an ambiguous side, and designers spend a lot of time quelling the anxiety that comes with financing a design project. The industry in general still struggles with how to deal with the sense that humans "use and are used by that technology," as design projects are often positioned to only deal with the first part of the statement: "humans use…" It takes a truly systemic approach to also design for how humans "are used by" technology. Many experience designers have latched on to the name "service design" to account for solutions that span objects and relationships; but at heart, experience design should do the same. There is nothing about experience design that implies the design of products and not services. Of course, this entire book is about how to design for the *experience of* an object or service.

This accountability for multistability is both the departure post-phenomenology experienced from classical phenomenology, and the key for the future of experience design. To cite Ihde again:

> A hammer is designed to do certain things—to drive nails into the shoemaker's shoe or into shingles on my shed, or to nail down a floor—but the design cannot prevent a hammer from becoming an objet d'art, a murder weapon, a paperweight, etc. Heidegger's insight was to have seen that an instrument *is what is does, and this in a context of assignments.* But he did not elaborate upon the multistable uses *any* technology can fall into with associated shifts in the complexities of 'assignments' as well. No technology is one thing, nor is it incapable of belonging to multiple contexts.[139]

The fundamental question of design metaphysics is what a design solution is, what it should be, and what it can be. A mobile device, as we have seen, can be many things: it *can be* a device for checking email, it *can be* a way to avoid other people, it *can be* a way to connect with other people, it *can be* a means of warding off boredom, and the list can go on. The device is not simply a device, and it is perfectly capable of serving many roles in different contexts. This question of what the solution or object *can be* is a phenomenological question that is of crucial importance for experience design. Concern with the *can be* is as fundamental to design as the future-facing nature of abductive thinking. The answer(s) will help set barriers around the sheer potentiality of how the solution is experienced and how to design for experience.

Part of this aim includes a post-phenomenological movement away from thinking about objects in terms of pure functionality. As Jean Baudrillard observes, "*'functional'* in no way qualifies what is adapted to a goal, *merely what is adapted to an order or system:* functionality is the ability to become integrated into an overall scheme. An object's functionality is the very thing that enables it to transcend its main 'function' in the direction of a secondary one, to play a part, to become a combining element, an adjustable item, within a universal system of signs."[140] Although certainly not a post-phenomenologist, Baudrillard contributed much to this current conversation with *System of Objects*—a text that touches on many different aspects of subject-object relations—with the guiding thread being how objects exist within a system of social relations. Thinking about consumer products, Baudrillard holds that each object has a functionality, but that functionality is precisely to transcend function and incorporate itself into a system in which it will have many functions. He comments that the system of objects is schizofunctional. Each object has a split functionality that allows it to serve many purposes according to the context of use.

The point here is not to paint a completely bleak picture of designer intention and multistability. Indeed, designers are already accounting for the multistable and schizofunctional nature of their solutions through practices such as rapid prototyping and constant revision. These practices are quite en vogue at the time of writing, and for good reason; they are excellent ways of meeting client demands for certainty and designer demands for exploration. "Taking an iterative approach" essentially tells a client that they will be involved in the design process to provide input along the way, solutions will be tested frequently, things will change based on client and/or user feedback received, and that there is no way to "get it right the first time." The client is essentially accepting that they are gaining certainty in the outcome be embracing uncertainty in the process. Similarly, "rapid prototyping" has reached full buzzword status in experience design communities, but again for good reason. While often bastardized to simply mean "do stuff quickly," the real goal of rapid prototyping is to obtain frequent user feedback and incorporate that feedback into future iterations, all while understanding that design solutions cannot be understood until put into practice. So again, clients are able to sacrifice certainty in the process to gain assurance in the "final" solution. The trouble is that rapid prototyping and human-centricity are often theoretical ideals that are not frequently practiced. Experience design, in a certain sense, is caught up in its own theoretical mode.

There is also a positive side of multistability and schizofunctionality for designers, as these effects are often the source of new design solutions. As Krippendorff notes:

> [P]ersonal computers (PCs) were born in the 1970s, when computers were largely mainframe, housed in cabinets behind climate controlled glass enclosures, and accessible only to designated operators. Designers combined two well-known ideal types, the typewriter and the television screen. Neither technology had much in common with computation. However, as metaphors, the typewriter plus TV screen enabled first designers but then more importantly, users, to draw upon experiences from these two well-understood empirical domains. The typewriter was known to produce text on paper; the television screen reproduced images electronically. Putting the TV screen on top of a typewriter suggested a new meaning, a paperless typewriter, one in which a text can be created character by character and scrolled up a screen, in a manner similar to the way that paper came out of a typewriter.[141]

The ability to remix objects within new use contexts provides the necessary flexibility for abductive thinking. While the typewriter and television had no inherent connection and served their own functions independently, their combination in a single design metaphor applied to a new context of use proved highly successful. So while multistability can hinder the designer's ability to instill a sense of certainty in his or her client, it also provides exciting sources of possibility. There is much value in the rearrangement of existing objects into new systems, which would not be possible without multistability. A strictly positivist view of technology would not allow such flexibility.

We have seen from the multistability discussion that creative misuse is a reaction against the act of design itself, and is enabled by the multistable nature of technology. Design theorist and general polymath Vilém Flusser wrote an essay on the word "design" in which he traced back some of its roots to deceit and trickery.[142] He noted that the machine is a device designed to trick the user and to cheat nature. The lever, for example, cheats gravity and tricks the user into a false sense of strength. Or as Tim Ingold puts it in his recent text:

Every object of design sets a trap by presenting a problem in the form of what appears to be its solution. Thus we are deceived into thinking of the spoon as a solution to the problem of how to transport food from bowl to mouth, when in fact it is the spoon that determines that we should do so rather than, say, holding the bowl directly to our lips. We are fooled into supposing that chairs afford the possibility to sit down, when it is the chair that dictates that we should sit rather than, say, squat. [...] As a creator or inventor of things, then, the designer is a trickster. Far from striving after perfection, his field is the management of imperfection.[143]

Interpreted in this way, experience design is a great imposition. Experience designers are literally invading the most personal, private phenomenon we have. Obviously, the designer's conscious aim is (hopefully) not to trick and deceive; but according to Flusser and Ingold, the effects of design result in a shift away from what we might call "natural" toward a mode of interaction determined, or at least heavily influenced, by someone else. Trickery occurs when the user forgets that their mode of interaction is designed and assumes it to be "natural." One might argue that creative misuse is a reaction against this heavy-handed designation that design imposes on the world. It is not a conscious reaction in the sense of protest; rather, it is a realization that a design solution is insufficient, therefore inciting the initiative to fix it, or at least decrease its imperfection.

Design theorists have called this type of effect "altruistic amateur designing," or when non-designers develop new uses for products and volunteer their time to communicate their new uses to others.[144] Each one of us develops new uses for existing products, whether we realize it or not. A simple search for what I assume to be a common problem for parents— a small child who managed to get chewing gum stuck in their hair—yields many home remedies using products with seemingly nothing to do with such a situation. The most popular seems to be applying peanut butter, which must break up the adhesive particles in the gum. Also included are cooking oil, petroleum jelly, and a strange combination of mouthwash and moisturizing lotion. All of these products have been appropriated from their original use and applied to a new context. These new uses can be read as backlash to designer intention and its inherent "trickery."

In light of these folk-knowledge examples, we must begin questioning the separation of designer, maker, and user:

[U]sers often use artifacts creatively. This may involve using something for a novel purpose – using a screwdriver to remove staples, for instance. Or it may involve some modification of the artifact to suit it for the novel purpose—filing down a key to make it more effective as a cutting instrument, for instance. Similarly, makers often construct creatively, departing from the instructions of designers in order to improve the artifact, or to continue construction in the absence of specified materials or needed tools. For example, cooks continually tinker with recipes to suit them to their own tastes, or substitute ingredients when specified ingredients are unavailable, prohibitively expensive, and so on. Phenomena like these show that although the roles of designer, maker, and user are distinguishable—even clearly and unequivocally distinguished in many cases—they are not rigorously distinct.[145]

It may be true that the role of designer and the act of designing are distinct; but in everyday practical situations, does that distinction matter? Are we abstracting design too much from the everyday? And are phenomena such as creative misuse showing us how these distinctions are perhaps only of theoretical value? Or, as Ingold asks: "If things are never finished—if the world is perpetually under construction by way of the activities of its inhabitants, who are tasked with keeping life going rather than bringing to completion projects specified at the outset—then can design any longer be distinguished from making?"[146] The spirit of design has been through much change in the last few centuries—from an esoteric, almost magical practice to a more mundane one. I believe that this is at least in part an effect of the recognition of creative misuse as an everyday occurrence.

What is becoming more apparent now is the power of the metaphysical shift in creative misuse. It is not simply that objects are used for other purposes but also that their cognitive designation—or perhaps, "mental model"—is changed to suit those new purposes: "[W]hen users manipulate artefacts in ways that are different to the use for which they was designed, we express this in terms of functions: if a screwdriver is used to extract small objects from cracks, we say that the user manipulates the screwdriver not as a 'screwdriver', but as a 'lever'."[147] Perhaps a more concrete example is the door stopper I use in my apartment. Like most extenement buildings in New York City, my floor is just slightly uneven, causing my bedroom door to sway half-closed, mostly due to the weight of belts and other things hanging on the back of the door (also a result of limited... rather, nonexistent storage and closet space). I began using a glass bottle to hold the door open. Realizing that the bottle alone was not heavy enough, I began filling it with change. In this example, the bottle has many purposes and many designations: it can simply be a bottle, or a change container, or a door stopper. The latter, in this case, is the most accurate since that is the primary function. We see a sort of hyper-praxical metaphysics of objects—the designation of a thing has little to do with its inherent properties but rather is determined by its use. The identity of the object is dependent on how it is used.

Another more personally embarrassing example of creative misuse—and also the dangers of when technology becomes "too embodied"—is a story of me burning myself with a kettle. I went through a phase of making pour-over coffee every morning. I enjoyed the ritual of grinding the beans, heating the water in the kettle, pouring it slowly over the grounds, etc. The only trouble with it is that it takes extra time, and being a stereotypical urban American who cannot go without stimulation for more than a few seconds, I would usually read a book while pouring the water. One morning, while engrossed in the book (held in one hand) and not paying much attention to the scalding hot water in the kettle (held in the other hand), my brain registered an itch on the side of my torso. Without consciously considering it, I lowered the kettle and used the spout to scratch the itch, thus accidentally pouring close-to-boiling water down the side of my body. About two years later, the physical scar remains. I have told this story before in reference to the dangers of creating completely "invisible" technology, but it also works to illustrate the sometimes completely subconscious ways we use technology for various purposes. At the moment my body experienced the itch, the object at hand (the kettle) ceased to be what it was and began to be *what it could do*. What is fascinating is that I did not consciously think "I can use this kettle spout to scratch my itch." If that were the case, I would have surely realized the danger. Instead, I subconsciously and intuitively came to know the object at hand according to *what it could do*—the interaction between the kettle and my body was solely based on the potential for action.

The literature on creative misuse is multifaceted, extending far beyond our present purpose. But the core message of misuse suggests that design extends itself outside of the studio and into everyday life, creating both a sense of incompleteness and blending of designer and maker. We are seeing a return to a craft-based mindset, in which designer and maker draw closer together. This is not to say the distinction is unimportant but simply that there is significant overlap. Creative misuse shows us that design does not end when a product or service is released into the world; users assume the role of designer and reinterpret the solution to better fit their purposes. If the distinctions between designers, makers, and users are less pronounced, then thinking in systems becomes so much more important. It isn't easy, but designers need to force themselves to consider the systematic change involved in their design decisions, and involve users in the process. This means that the experience of design solutions is of tantamount importance to the act of designing, and we therefore need a better understanding of the experience of these solutions.

Objects, Things, Interactions, and Experiences

The complexity of experience design lies in its attempt to do what its name implies: to design experiences. We can design objects according to intention, constraints, specifications, etc., but the experience of those objects is always idiosyncratic and inherently subjective. The previous discussions have shown that experience is always *of something*, in the sense that we cannot simply "experience" just as we cannot simply "be conscious"—there is always a focal point. If this is the case, then designing an experience is dependent on designing the objects of experience.

This view, however, is a bit too simplistic, as it fails to account for the intangibility inherent within many, if not all, design practices. We have seen thus far how post-phenomenology moves past Heidegger's original conception of interaction to a more "thingly" notion of being. Multistability, intention, and mediation have shown the complexity of characterizing objects, but we have not yet given sufficient attention to the nature of things as it relates to their design.

Prasad Boradkar provides a fantastic summary of the history of things and how humans have philosophized about them.[148] Dating all the way back to around 600 B.C.E., pre-Socratic philosophers Thales, Anaximander, and Anaximenes conceived of the world as composed of some kind of basic material. Others like Heraclitus focused on fire as the primary element, while Pythagoras suggested numbers and proportions were the basic material of things. Parmenides argued that reality was not knowable at all, and what we saw as reality was an illusion. Plato argued for ideal forms, or the notion that our reality of things is simply an imitation of some greater reality in which pure objects exist. Fast-forward to around

1640 and Descartes tells us that the mind and thought compose reality, and Leibniz conceives the monad as a spiritual, omnipresent, ghostly material of reality. Immanuel Kant then posits that our knowledge of the world is not necessarily limited by our sense organs, and Hegel asserts that knowledge of things is simply the knowledge of their properties. Heidegger returned to Greek thought to establish the thing as that which gathers meaning. From here, we arrive at a modern philosophy of things we have seen via Latour, Verbeek, Ihde, and others.

This comically short history of thinking about things shows the depth and breadth of opinion on how we make sense of the world of things. Instead of covering this vast expanse, the goal here is to show progression from phenomenology to post-phenomenology with regard to thinking about things. Heidegger's focus on things came later in his career, with a larger turning of attention to technology. This is the point at which post-phenomenologists pick up Heidegger's thought and more fully articulate a theory of things. To continue this line of thought, I'd like to spend the rest of this chapter discussing Heidegger's conception of a thing as it relates to post-phenomenology and design

A key point we have made about experience design is its intangibility. We can take the *designing of experiences* quite literally to mean that designers are creating conditions that influence experience on an individual level. While ideally accurate, this view lends itself to all types of criticism, much of which we covered in sections on intentionality and multistability. How can we actually design individual interpretation of an experience with any kind of validity? Perhaps we cannot. What is more clear, however, is that humans experience systems of objects, not individual, isolated things. Here, we have another paradox: if experience design is designing an experience, but we can only design experiences via things, then experience design is always stuck in a hermeneutic circle of applying design to both tangible things and intangible systems, never knowing which comes first. One thing we might say is that experience design is not concerned with the design of objects as such, but rather of the effects that these objects have on intangible systems.

We might begin to make sense of this paradox by returning to Heidegger's discussion of things. Heidegger describes the thing as not an object but rather a process when he states that "[t]he jug is a thing insofar as it things" and that "[t]hinging is the nearing of the world."[149] Returning to the Greek origins, the word "thing" means "gathering," or the bringing together of disparate meaning. The jug gathers functionality as a vessel to hold wine; it gathers cultural meaning as a vessel used in ceremony, ritual, or religious service; it gathers familial meaning when used for a family dinner; and it gathers destructive power when used as a weapon. The thing operates to gather and present this meaning to be interpreted. "The jug's essential nature, its presencing, so experienced and thought of in these terms, is what we call thing."[150] In this way, the object is the materiality of what is encountered, and the thing is the interpretation of that materiality in context. This interpretation is not simply an act of determining meaning from a material object, but rather an interaction between the tangible, material aspects of the object and its immaterial qualities:

> We become aware of the vessel's holding nature when we fill the jug. The jug's bottom and sides obviously take on the task of holding. But not so fast! When we fill the jug with wine, do we pour the wine into the sides and bottom? At most, we pour the wine between the sides and over the bottom. Sides and bottom are, to be sure, what is impermeable in the vessel. But what is impermeable is not yet what does the holding. When we fill the jug, the pouring that fills it flows into the empty jug. The emptiness, the void, is what does the vessel's holding. The empty space, this nothing of the jug, is what the jug is as the holding vessel.[151]

Interpretation of functionality is a result of the material and immaterial; the stuff and the void. The unseen aspects of the thing or system—the emptiness, the void—are what give shape to that which is designed. Experience design, then, must be concerned with the tangible and the intangible, specifically the interaction between them. As Mads Folkmann points out, "both material and immaterial effects are involved when design (objects, solutions, services) enters the human domain of creating and evoking meaning. They become part of the aesthetic, thus part of the overall process of the distribution of meaning by means of aestheticization—both by a sensual staging of experience and by shaping the discursive and informational setting of knowledge and meaning."[152] Thus, we might say that experience design challenges aesthetics to include both non-conscious experience and conscious interpretation. Even if we cannot truly *design an experience*, we can certainly take care in considering intangible systems of meaning.

Bruno Latour sees this dichotomy slightly differently—as one of material versus design, in which objects reside within a material realm and things are composed of designed artifacts:

> If it is true as I have claimed that we have never been modern, and if it is true, as a consequence, that 'matters of fact' have now clearly become 'matters of concern', then there is logic to the following observation: the typically modernist divide between materiality on the one hand and design on the other is slowly being dissolved away. The more objects are turned into things—that is, the more matters of facts are turned into matters of concern—the more they are rendered into objects of design through and through.[153]

Latour hits on an interesting progression here from object to thing, and perhaps back to object. If a key distinction between object and thing is a sense of meaningful interpretation, then we might add to that distinction by referring back to Heidegger's thoughts on foreground and background relations implicit with the present-at-hand and ready-to-hand discussion. The thing "things" by presenting itself as a meaningful entity, but it also incorporates itself into the background when "object-ed." An object becomes a thing when pointed to, when one says "this thing," and becomes background when not identified. We might also say that the meaning of a thing is usually tied to its use contexts and the ways it mediates. For example, a mobile device quickly becomes a meaningful messenger when it vibrates with a text, and then turns back into an object when returned to one's pocket. But one might also argue that the consciousness of the object's thing-ness brings it back to objective awareness. The movement back and forth is unending.

In his theory of things, Bill Brown adds a bit more nuance to this object-thing distinction:

> [W]e look through objects (to see what they disclose about history, society, nature, or culture-above all, what they disclose about us), but we only catch a glimpse of things. We look through objects because there are codes by which our interpretive attention makes them meaningful, because there is a discourse of objectivity that allows us to use them as facts. A thing, in contrast, can hardly function as a window. We begin to confront the thingness of

objects when they stop working for us: when the drill breaks, when the car stalls, when the windows get filthy, when their flow within the circuits of production and distribution, consumption and exhibition, has been arrested, however momentarily.[154]

The thing-ness of things for Brown is inherently tied to its functionality. The thing might gather and present meaning in a certain way, but it does so in a way that diverts attention from itself as a thing, as the presentation as thing comes in the form of breakage. The thing fails to perform its function, and the user is aware of it as such. It's the "don't look down" equivalent of everyday life—skilled interactions often involve a purposeful lack of conscious deliberation. If you think too hard about drinking from a cup, you'll probably spill on yourself. Its meaning as a cup is not to be reflected upon while enacting its functionality.

The important question for designers is where this meaning comes from and how to design with it. How might designers treat meaning as a material within the design process, and not necessarily work against it but work within it? Can meaning function like grooves in the wood shaped by a craftsperson, which provide natural direction the designer can work *with* instead of *against*? Heidegger notes that "[t]he jug is not a vessel because it was made; rather, the jug had to be made because it is this holding vessel."[155] The designed thing serves a purpose, coming into being in order to serve that purpose as opposed to the other way around. Experience designers, then, are the ones discovering those purposes and attempting to understand both the conditions of purpose and the potential variation of introducing a new thing into the existing system. The processes of designing and making do not create the thing as we know it but rather create its objective qualities: "The making, it is true, lets the jug come into its own. But that which in the jug's nature is its own is never brought about by its making. Now released from the making process, the self-supporting jug has to gather itself for the task of containing. In the process of its making, of course, the jug must first show its outward appearance to the maker."[156] But Heidegger forgets a couple of key points here: 1) We can design at a systems level, influencing how the thing *things*. And 2) the object does not simply exist apart from the maker as a gathering of meaning and intent; it *things* on its own with multistable tendencies that influence its function across contexts. This is where post-phenomenology picks up the analysis to show radical variability in object use. It is also where experience designers tend to play, navigating this variability and complexity to design the intangible.

Chapter 6
Embodiment and Meaning Formation

Embodiment

"Machines are simulated organs of the human body."[157]

As mentioned in chapter 2, Heideggerian phenomenology can be read as a reaction to Cartesian dualism. Instead of relying on a strict separation of mind and body, Heidegger wanted to show how the two are intrinsically linked, and their relationship is not hierarchical. Cartesian dualism has permeated many aspects of our culture far beyond purely philosophical considerations—from the separation of physical and mental health to distinctions between theory and practice. More recently, cognitive scientists have begun to realize that their entire field has been built on this dualist assumption, and articulated new ways to think about how mind and body co-construct and rely on one another. We will cover some aspects of embodied cognition, as the new field is often called, but the focus is on the concept of embodiment as it relates to design theory and the formation of meaning systems. What does it mean to be embodied in a specific context and experience it from within?

When dealing with a question this large, it is necessary to shed ourselves of some less-than-helpful assumptions. The first assumption I see designers make all the time is that users are rational subjects. Of course, this assumption is implicit in actions, though not necessarily conscious in thoughts. A second related assumption is that users are conscious of their own goals; they perform actions based on ends they consciously seek to meet. And finally, a third related assumption is that users think *then* act—users identify a goal, determine a cognitive plan of action, and then execute that action. Many of the outputs of experience design rest on these assumptions, from flow diagrams to persons to scenarios and use cases. These outputs are important and necessary, but the point here is that without recognition of their inherently disembodied state, they can often lead designers down an unnecessarily dualist path.

Many design practices fall into these dualist traps. It is not the fault of design but rather a testament to how ingrained Cartesianism is within most of Western culture. Cognitive scientists have been working on ways to break out of this paradigm, mostly under the umbrella of embodied cognition, or the idea that thinking is embodied in the world; we do not formulate theoretical models of the world and then act on them, but rather we interact with things and learn, thus shaping our future behavior. Andy Clark explains how this view allows us to think about knowledge in a radically different way: "Intelligence and understanding are rooted not in the presence and manipulation of explicit, language-like data structures, but in something more earthy: the tuning of basic responses to a real world that enables an embodied organism to sense, act, and survive."[158] Take the example of education. The older model of education says that route memorization is the only way for students to commit facts into long term memory. This is, however, only one type of knowing. Real understanding comes from acting out what we know by *experiencing* it in a way that our bodily engagement facilitates understanding. The old adage of "learn by doing" rings true. Or the old quote attributed to Miles Kingston, "Knowledge is knowing a tomato is a fruit, wisdom is not putting in a fruit salad" is accurate because it acknowledges the role of experience in wisdom and understanding. Facts alone can be useful, but they are no substitute for experience. Knowledge tells us how to classify something, such as a tomato, while understanding suggests how we can use it. Embodied cognition, at a high level, is simply the acknowledgement of context, experience, and praxis—something that traditional cognitive science and philosophy did not historically do.

In chapter 2, we mentioned Hubert Dreyfus's work on artificial intelligence but did not go into much detail about the peripheral effects of what he suggested. In challenging artificial intelligence (AI) researchers to think beyond a dualist model of the mind and body, Dreyfus was critiquing the entire project of cognitive science to date. In a sense, his work is not simply a critique of AI—it represents a theory of embodied, contextual, and praxis-based cognition that happens to use AI (a very convenient example for a philosopher at MIT) as its core example. Dreyfus argued that classical AI was based on symbolic systems that ignored bodily context.[159] In other words, a computer, at least at the time, was not able to adapt to changing environmental conditions because it had no bodily experience. In addition, the goal at the time was to create AI that thinks and behaves like a human. But Dreyfus argues that humans do not engage with the world based on discrete sets of facts that can be translated into code. Instead, he took a Heideggerian approach and asserted that humans are bound within their context, and that situational elements affect behavior and cognition more so than the facts we can recite. For example, we know that tomatoes are fruit, but because of contextual factors such as what might taste good in combination with other fruits, they are not included in a fruit salad. The fact that they belong in the fruit category is trumped by the implicit understanding of how they operate in combination with other fruits. We see this play out constantly in the interaction design and information architecture contexts.[160] A piece of web content might fit logically under one category, but according to the behavioral patterns of users, it might fit better under another label. For example, the IRS website might file a tax form under Taxes > Forms > Individuals > [form]. However, when following the goals users have on the site, they might house common tax forms under a label that reads something like "I need to do my taxes." There is a difference between what the content *is* and what is allows users to *do*.

Much of this conversation is contingent on ideas of the body and embodiment, which is the focus of much of Maurice Merleau-Ponty's work. Merleau-Ponty was a French phenomenologist and contemporary of Heidegger who placed his attention on the role of the body in perception and cognition. We can think of the body as a physical thing in space but also as an effect of having the physical-spatial thing: "For Merleau-Ponty, the body is neither subject nor object, but an ambiguous third party. Nonetheless, the body plays a critical role in any theory of perception. Perception of an external reality comes about through and in relation to a sense of the body." A theory of the body, Merleau-Ponty argued, "is already a theory of perception"[161] Herein lies the intimate relationship between experience design and interaction design. The body for interaction design is concentrated on physical sensation—seeing, hearing, feeling, etc.—while experience design might be more focused on the effect that the body has in terms of how the individual experiences that with which one interacts.

Merleau-Ponty also adopted a particularly anti-dualist stance to mind and world: "According to Merleau-Ponty, as an agent acquires skills, those skills are 'stored,' not as representations in the agent's mind, but as the solicitations of situations in the world. What the learner acquires through experience is not represented at all but is presented to the learner as more and more finely discriminated situations."[162] He argued against the idea that our primary means of understanding the world is by representing it in our minds. Instead, the world is constantly presenting itself to the individual in new ways, and much of our memory stores are external to the mind and accessed through the body and adapted to changing contexts. Philosophers of technology have cited phenomena and objects such as hard drives literally storing "memory" and mobile devices decreasing the need to memorize phone numbers. This memory is stored in the environment, not in our minds. Even analog things like maps and written instructions serve to guide behavior but are not necessarily stored as mental representations; we access them only when needed, and always through the body. This theory of mind is often referred to as extended mind, which holds that the function of the mind is not contained within the head but extends out into the world, while still inherently connected to the body.[163]

Given the extension of the mind into the world, making sense of the things with which we interact becomes less dependent on what these things objectively *are,* and more on what they can *do.* Returning to the tax form example above, while the metaphysical existence of the form is simply a page with words and text boxes, what the user does with it is often more meaningful and useful. Merleau-Ponty asserted that this is true of our entire conception of the body: "What counts for the orientation of the spectacle is not my body as it in fact is, as a thing in objective space, but as a system of possible actions, a virtual body withe its phenomenal 'place' defined by its task and situation. My body is wherever there is something to be done."[164] The body as a "system of possible actions" has major implications for experience design, perhaps most importantly dealing with the role of user goals and the multistability of technology. The key question becomes: can we design a system that guides the accomplishment of goals, some conscious and some non-conscious, all within the bounds of multistability? In other words, is it possible to account for all this contextual variability with a design solution?

Thinkers such as Bonsiepe have taken a very literal approach to the body's role in design, claiming that all design is associated with attaching tools to the body: "It may be maintained that all design ultimately ends in the body. Perceptual space occupies a prime position, because people are first and foremost creatures with eyes. In the case of tools—both material and immaterial (software) tools—the task of design is to attach the artifacts to the human body. That process is described by the term 'structural coupling.'"[165] The structural coupling Bonsiepe describes is quite literally taking a piece of technology as an appendage. The mobile phone becomes an extension of the brain just like a hand axe is an extension of the hand and arm. We saw this in the previous example of Beckett's Malone and his objects. The stick especially serves an extension of the arm, or in his case, a substitute for a body that is no longer functional enough to operate on its own. In many cases, designers are certainly concerned with augmenting the physical body, and one might argue in all cases, even with intangible software, that they are extending the body's capacity beyond its own physical limits. Through Google Street View, we can "see" places that we are not currently located. And, through a multitude of communication technologies, we are able to extend the voice beyond the auditory capacities of others. The caveat here is of course that even with all that these technologies enable, they also obscure. As Don Ihde noted, the telescope allows us to see further than we naturally can, but it also obscures what is close by. It is no different for digital technology.

Affordances and Action

The notion that our actions and cognitions are embodied in certain contexts is familiar to most designers, although perhaps not as ingrained as one would like. Modern designers are still afflicted with the same deep-seated dualist bias that affected early AI researchers (and still does to a large extent). The difference is that embodiment theories are becoming more embedded into our conception of the world, so there is a more balanced and shared view of the individual. In other words, as we have mentioned before, there is a difference between most individual experience designers' metaphysical understanding of the world on a conscious and non-conscious level. Outwardly, one would never argue that users act based solely on mental representations to formulate a plan of action and then execute that action in the world. But in the embodied expression of their work, the dualist tendencies bubble up.

When Merleau-Ponty states that "my body is wherever there is something to be done," he places what we might call the body-effect, or the experience of the body, into the "earthy" realm, which Andy Clark describes as the site of cognition. Body and mind come together perhaps most explicitly in what we call *experience*. This earthy place is the site of potentialities, in which the individual is constantly mediating between which actions are possible and preferable, reading cues from the environment and their own body to influence their decisions. Consider the rudimentary example of someone standing at the top of a staircase with the goal of descending the stairs. One possible action is to simply walk down the stairs. Another is to creatively misuse the hand rail and slide down it. If the individual is a healthy teenager, both actions are possible; and depending on whether an implicit goal is to descend the stairs in a creative manner, one might be preferable over the other. If the individual is an 80-year-old with arthritis who uses a cane to walk, one possibility is completely out of the question, while the other will be difficult but still possible.

Chapter 3 showed the importance of the hands for how humans interact with their worlds. Almost all action, certainly any action involved in design, is done through the hands. Thus, hands are the active agents of potentiality; they are how we play out the possibilities of our world. But the rest of the body, as we saw in the elderly individual in the previous example, limits the performance of the hands and thus limits creative misuse. Embodiment can enable or hinder creative misuse by limiting the possibilities that objects afford. Once again we see body, mind, and world coming together in an emergent system. As Franssen noted, objects have a *for-ness*—a reason for being that calls forth certain actions. But these potential actions are limited by bodily capacity and opened up by creative misuse, resulting in a constant struggle and mediation between what can theoretically be done and what can practically be done.

In the discussion of Latour's work, it was mentioned that designers create scripts, or intended/planned actions or purposes for an object. The speed bump is embedded with a script that allows it to function as an object that slows cars, similar to something like Facebook having the (apparent) script to (re)connect people who are unable to socialize in person. Designers create these scripts by embedding and making clear affordances to communicate the possibilities of use. Many designers are familiar with the concept of affordances via Don Norman's classic text *The Design of Everyday Things*, in which he articulates affordances as elements of an interface that communicate what can be done:

doorknobs afford *graspability* and *turnability*, buttons on a digital interface afford *pushability*, chairs afford *sitability*. For most purposes, this simple definition is sufficient—designers can understand their work as the process of creating clear affordances that communicate potential action. But the theory of affordances runs deeper than communication; it points to a fundamental blending of the physical and cognitive.

Flusser remarks that "an 'object' is what gets in the way, a problem thrown in your path like a projectile (coming as it does from the Latin objectum, Greek problema)."[166] We might interpret the object, especially the designed object, as something that impedes as much as it improves, essentially driving the user further from his or her end goal by serving as an intermediary. With objects "in the way," users are more prone to mistakes. However, I'm not so sure we can take Flusser's etymological interpretation too literally, as designed objects have become so ingrained into our everyday being. Instead, it is more useful to consider how designed objects create a system of interaction, and within that system, how affordances are made apparent and how users are interpreting them.

The theory of affordances has its origins with James J. Gibson, a psychologist who studied airplane cockpits, particularly how pilots interact with these highly complex interfaces. Gibson noted that the pilots' behavior is similar to our everyday interaction with objects in the sense that we do not perceive objects as discrete things, at least not at first. Rather, we perceive objects according to their possible actions. We perceive the steering wheel in a car primarily as something we can grasp, especially when the wheel has grooves for our fingers to fit inside, and secondarily as a means of pointing the car in a certain direction. The steering wheel affords *graspability* and *steerability*. Only after that perception do we think of it as a "steering wheel," and our name for it is completely arbitrary in terms of what it actually does. In this way, the theory of affordances is a framework for understanding objects not simply by *what they are* but also, and primarily, by *what they do*.

Gibson used his concept of affordance to critique dualism in a very similar manner to Heidegger and Merleau-Ponty. He saw affordances as evidence against the hard line drawn between self and world:

> When in use, a tool is a sort of extension of the hand, almost an attachment to it or part of the user's own body, and thus no longer a part of the environment of the user. But when not in use the tool is simply a detached object of the environment, graspable and

portable, to be sure, but nevertheless external to the observer. This capacity to attach something to the body suggests that the boundary between the animal and the environment is not fixed at the surface of the skin but can shift. More generally it suggests that the absolute duality of 'objective' and 'subjective' is false. When we consider the affordances of things, we escape this philosophical dichotomy.[167]

In a certain sense, Gibson is making up for some of the shortcomings that post-phenomenology pointed out in Heidegger's work, namely the lack of consideration for individual objects. Gibson's account of the object in use as being completely embodied seems quite similar to Heidegger's notion of readiness-to-hand. The object blends into the background and ceases to be an object of consideration. When not in use, Gibson says the object becomes detached from the body and assumes a sort of present-at-hand status as an external, observable thing. However, the ability to perceptually attach an object to the body, or to structurally couple them, is evidence for Gibson that categories such as subject and object are unnecessarily restrictive and not completely accurate. Embodied action or skillful manipulation couples body and world into a system of interaction. An expert graphic designer is coupled with the mouse/trackpad/stylus when creating a design in Photoshop—and perhaps in instances of deep expertise, they are coupled with Photoshop itself, manipulating the interface without conscious thought—working toward the end goal of a final design. The mouse/trackpad/stylus is literally an extension of the hand.

Given the action-oriented status of affordances, the concept itself resists categorical classification. As Gibson points out:

> An important fact about the affordances of the environment is that they are in a sense objective, real, and physical, unlike values and meanings, which are often supposed to be subjective, phenomenal, and mental. But, actually, an affordance is neither an objective property nor a subjective property; or it is both if you like. An affordance cuts across the dichotomy of subjective-objective and helps us to understand its inadequacy. It is equally a fact of the environment and a fact of behavior. It is both physical and psychical, yet neither. An affordance points both ways, to the environment and to the observer.[168]

The point here is a bit convoluted but important. When we talk about affordances as cues that communicate action, we are automatically placing them into an external or objective category. The affordance associated with a button on a website is not simply a result of its look and feel—i.e., that it "looks" like a user can press it. The affordance is a result of sensory communication, interpretation, and potential action. As a potential for action, we cannot classify affordances as purely mental interpretations, physical properties, a little of both, or neither. In other words, affordances call for an entirely new way°of thinking about our relation to objects. By affording action, affordances are pure potentiality, which both communicate and enable action.

If we trace the roots back before Gibson, we can see similar sentiments in Georg Simmel's study of art.[169] Using a decorative vase as an example, Simmel notes that a key difference between art and practical objects is the latter's ability to communicate its potential use—in this case, via the vase's handle. Simmel states: "[N]ot only must it be possible for the handle actually to perform its practical function, but the possibility must also be manifest in its appearance, and empathetically so in the case of apparently soldered handles, as opposed to those apparently shaped in one movement with the body of the vase."[170] Beyond a study of art and practical objects, Simmel is making a statement on the differentiation of art and design: an artistic vase might have a handle just like a practically designed vase, but the communication of how to grab and hold the former is less crucial than the latter. The designed vase, which includes handles that were not shaped with the body of the vase but rather soldered on, must communicate its use in order to be practical. We might say that design, for Simmel, is the act of communicating practical use. Simmel goes on to discuss how the handle represents the vase's "reaching out" into the world and its connection to human teleology, much like Gibson on affordances.

Gibson might argue that the affordance exists regardless of the bodily capability of the perceiver, but in a practical sense, the object's potential for action must be considered alongside bodily capability. In the staircase example above, the handrail affords *slideability* for both the teenager and the arthritic 80-year-old, but only the former is able to complete the afforded action. This brings up the difference between the perception of an affordance and the ability to act on it. Perception is almost universal, with the exception of certain culturally determined affordances and differing bodily ability, whereas the utility of the affordance is completely dependent on bodily capacity. We do not see the kind of structural coupling discussed earlier without the capacity to act, as the action itself creates the coupling. Affordances communicate the verb— the action word or phrase that allows the user to determine an object's script—such as a steering wheel is used to steer. But they might also serve the opposite function of communicating potentialities for creative misuse, as they introduce non-designers to their capacity for future thinking:

> An affordance is an 'actual possibility', a 'promised action opportunity.' Affordances are the result of interactional perceptions, seeing not just a feature, but a future way of making use of that feature. The key to understanding an affordance is to realise its utterly unsemiotic nature; affordances are the opposite of digital communications needing decoding. If they are communications, they are direct communications, without mediation, communications, as it were, between things and my body without the involvement of my mind. I do not see a shape, but a handle, or rather a 'handlable'; I see myself handling that shape; or more precisely, my hand sees that handlable, reaching out for it before I have even really 'seen' it (as if I were something other than my hand).[171]

Affordances communicate the need for future thinking. A user perceives an affordance immediately as what might happen in the future, such as using a steering wheel to keep a car on the road. But one can also think of misuses for the steering wheel, from something to tap on while listening to their favorite song or to purposefully take the car off the road in order to avoid hitting a child in the street. In these moments, the steering wheel's affordance communicates instantly. We might think of the affordance as forced abductive thinking: it forces the user to think about *what could be* and what an object *can do*, rather than what exists now. As mentioned a few times before, everyone designs but not everyone is a designer. We all interact with and perceive affordances; it is the resulting action that designates design.

In the earlier passage, Tonkinwise also mentions that affordances communicate "between things and my body without the involvement of my mind," which points out the essential between-ness of affordances, as what Gibson refers to as "both physical and psychical, yet neither."

Krippendorff also noted that "Gibson recognized the need for a human-centered language that would neither physicalize human perception [...] nor psychologize the terrestrial environment."[172] The special quality of affordances is that they resist objective or subjective categories, and thus can operate outside the bounds of dualism. I believe design can build off this resistance to categorization to rethink the role of the verb, or the role that action plays in both design and use. Instead of explaining what designed objects *are*, we can articulate what it means for designed objects *to be*. We can move from a metaphysics of design to the phenomenology of design.

Embodied Meaning

Part of this movement from *what things are* to *what things do*, or what we might call an action-oriented understanding of designed objects, requires a deeper understanding of how meaning operates in the designed world. The following will not be a broad overview of meaning but rather a more focused examination of meaning in the designed world, and how embodiment and affordances contribute to meaning creation. As we will see, meaning is almost the opposing force of design; it reflects the successes and failures of the design process, depending on the designer's intent and the user's interpretation.

The notion of "embodied meaning" holds that meaning "arises from the ways in which we engage with and act within the world."[173] So this highly personal concept of meaning is actually distributed around the environment and is contingent on interaction with things. For example, a brain in a vat—the hyperbolic but still accurate portrayal of the ends of artificial intelligence—would not have a sense of meaning, since despite its ability to store and recite facts, it has no bodily engagement with the world. Sensemaking and learning are dependent on things like memory and access to information, but they are also dependent on the potential for action. There was university professor I knew while in college who was able to retain information much like a machine. Before I took any of his classes, he seemed like an extremely well-read, articulate, and highly intelligent person, at least in casual social situations. While taking one of his graduate level classes, however, I realized that his strength as a scholar did not extend beyond having an efficient long-term memory. He could recite passages, name the date and publisher of every text he mentioned, and sum up major theorists' work in a few sentences; yet, he was unable to go any further to articulate a strong argument based on what he knew (which is ironic for a literary theorist). The point here is not to pick on him—surely we all have struggled with similar instances, not being able to push further than *what we know now* (writing this book has provided more than my fair share). The point is that his sense of meaning in each of the texts was not embodied; he read them many times but did not *do* anything with them.

Action is incredibly important for designers as they attempt to embody knowledge and understanding. Common design practices such as sketching and prototyping are excellent ways to enact theoretical knowledge, but I've found that many designers fail to recognize the importance of writing. I see writing as an intermediary between decontextualized, armchair-style thinking and full prototyping. It allows a designer to consciously articulate intentions, scenarios, and possible outcomes by crafting a linear story in which one can easily see missing pieces or conflicting messages. For example, on a surface level, we can understand Freudian psychoanalysis as a process of making the unconscious conscious. The therapeutic environment is designed to identify the patient's unconscious desires as the source of neurosis, and since the unconscious is essentially anti-rational and unknown, analysis aims to bring these desires into consciousness, slowly and carefully, so they can be rationally examined. Eventually, the goal is to assist the patient in analyzing these desires to discover why they are causing neuroses, and through this surfacing and realization, the patient will experience a decrease in symptoms. It brings the source of neurosis from the decontextualized, disembodied unconscious into the embodied conscious mind through acting out, repetition, etc. There are certainly some important differences between designers and patients undergoing psychoanalysis (although perhaps not as many as we think), the act of doing something with knowledge carries over to the design process.

In the design process and in everyday life, meaning must be approached from a systems perspective. It's obvious that meaning is never divorced from its context. For example, we cannot understand the interior of a coffee shop without also understanding its relation to tables, chairs, coffee, customers; we cannot understand an automobile without also understanding its relation to roads, drivers, cities, and highways. Phenomenology is interested in the nature of the world, but always through the lens of the individual and their capacity to generate meaning. That interpretation—the finding of place, understanding the connection between self and world—is experience. Designed objects can either help us understand the complex web of meaning in which we exist, or they can obscure it, or both.

Klaus Krippendorff spent much of his career mapping out how designed objects incorporate themselves into everyday life and become meaningful. He called the practice "product semantics," and aimed to position his study as a next evolution of design thinking, which until then has concentrated on the design process itself and how designers think, often forgetting the effects of designed objects. In this sense, product semantics begins to unpack some of the things we've alluded to so far—namely, that design practice is only half of a comprehensive design theory.

> Product semantics should be concerned not with the forms, surfaces and visual or tactile boundaries of artifacts (the things that can be photographed and shown in design exhibits), but with the understanding that penetrates them. Product semantics should be concerned not with material objects as such, but with how they participate in human affairs, how they support understanding and practice. Product semantics should optimize not performance, as measured by outside criteria, but meaningfulness, motivation and the centeredness of humans in their world by their own criteria.[174]

Product semantics is a bit different from the study of objects in the sense that it emphasizes meaning systems over physicality. Product semantics might look at something like a water bottle, ignoring its physical qualities and design, and concentrate on what the ubiquity of portable bottles means for environmental concerns; how the bottle mediates the relationship between humans and their own bodily needs; and how buying one brand of water over another communicates certain qualities of the purchaser. It would also be concerned with the use practices of objects, such as the difference between buying personal water bottles and choosing to carry refillable bottles. "Understanding things involves relating them to their context of use, to their practice, including to other things we are aware of. Artifacts take part in and well designed artifacts support circular enabling patterns involving our actions on them, our perceptions of them and what we intend to accomplish with them."[175]

Carrying drinking water, of course, accomplishes the initial goal of staying hydrated. However, product semantics begins to blend with branding and design research by examining the differing experience and communication of buying expensive imported water versus buying a refillable metal bottle versus refilling previously-purchased plastic bottles. Understanding these products in use allows us to make inferences about the nature of these differences. Imported water likely communicates a certain social status and ostensible concern with the quality of water (imported is somehow better). Refilling a metal bottle communicates a mix of environmental concern by not wasting multiple plastic bottles, economic concern over the cost of buying water every day, health concern about the chemicals from plastic bottles that supposedly leech into water, and the willingness to pay more money up front in order to save money later. Finally, refilling a cheap plastic bottle communicates a concern for both environment and cost, without being willing to spend the necessary money for a reusable bottle. Each of these permutations create a different system of meaning, both in terms of how others perceive the user and how the user behaves toward their own thirst. Carrying water also assumes that the user desires constant hydration, is likely not in a place where free, quality water is available throughout the day, and is willing to carry the weight of water with them. These meanings also change across contexts, from bringing water to work, to the gym, or sneaking it into a movie theater so as not to pay higher prices. These are all initial assumptions that can be validated through contextual research into the semantics of water bottles with the aim of understanding how carrying water makes sense in certain situations. The goal of product semantics is to fully articulate these meaning systems, both from the user's and the observer's perspectives.

It is easy to fall into various levels of vague description when talking about meaning. While I'm not sure we can completely avoid that here, we can add a bit of specificity in terms of the difference between sense and meaning. Krippendorff describes the difference in terms of use context: "We say that something makes sense when we understand the role it plays in a particular context, when we have a satisfactory explanation of what it does. In contrast, the meaning of an object is the sum total of all the contexts for which someone is capable of imagining some sense for it. In short something means (or enables someone to see or anticipate) its possible contexts of use."[176] It is a difference of use cases. Sense relates to one use case whereas meaning is associated with a larger system of sensemaking that accounts for multiple contexts of use. In the water bottle example, we might say that the bottle makes sense as a vessel for holding water and is designed in order to afford portability and drinkability. Its meaning, however, speaks to the larger communication systems associated with which type of water it is and how it is used across contexts. In one context, it might simply be a vessel. In another, it might be something used to occupy the hands when nervous, such as when speaking in public. Meaning is also dependent on abduction. It necessitates an orientation toward potential use cases and systems of signification around future contexts.

Practices such as service design, strategic design, and systemic design have specifically called out the need for considering broad meaning systems, even in the most hyper-focused design activities. The question remains, however, how these disciplines are different from experience design. The failure of experience design is the inability for many practitioners to differentiate between the interaction and the experience of an interaction. We might design the interaction with a water bottle: how it fits within the hand, size of the spout, size of the bottle, etc. But the experience of the bottle extends beyond tangible features of the bottle and into how the bottle makes sense in certain situations—how it fits into a larger system of meaning centered around the use of the bottle. Part of the power that experience design has is fitting individual sense to systemic meaning. "We always make sense of our practice with things but, as we generalize these experiences to the meanings of things and apply these meanings as guides for our practice of living with things, we inevitably organize the ecology that surround us."[177] We naturally organize meaning ecosystems, but experience design makes this process explicit. It takes the embodied practice of organizing everyday life and abstracts it just enough to make it conscious.

Experience design is inherently complex because of its concern with the nodes in a system of meaning. "The truth of a text is always secondary to its reading, just as the use of an artifact is always secondary to its meanings."[178] A text that is read in the traditional sense is always read from the perspective of an individual, so its first interaction happens from the point of view of one. Any sense of truth (and truth is probably the wrong word) must come after the moment of encounter when a text is read. We *read* objects in a similar way as we do texts. Therefore, it seems to make little sense when Krippendorff asserts "the use of an artifact is always secondary to its meanings." The first part of his statement sets up interaction to precede interpretation, but the second part reverses his logic. Surely texts and objects exist in the same overall cultural system of meaning. What I believe he is getting at is that the use of an object is necessary for sensemaking, not necessarily for meaning, since meaning is, or at least can be, distinct from individual sense. We know the meaning of a military tank even though we probably have not operated one. But without that practical perspective, the tank makes little sense.

Meaning, then, has a certain reliance on communication. Without the ability to communicate sense through language, design would remain confined to an individual or to a small number of individuals in a small geographical area who share the same language. This is the type of sense that existed in craft societies—small networks of individuals with little to no distinction between maker, designer, and user. Any sense of a meaning system was relatively confined and was mostly determined by individuals within villages. But we should be careful to not relegate language and communication to the simple conveying of information. Certainly, the passing of ideas is a large part of linguistic systems, but language also has a more active quality of not only describing reality, but also creating reality.[179] Krippendorff uses Wittgenstein's ideas on language games and incorporates them into the discussion on design: "Language does not represent, it does something, and the criterion of its use is not truth but its appropriateness, what makes it the right thing to say in a given circumstance, and what makes it meaningful to the participants—as judged by the participants in the language game."[180] The ways that we create meaning through language are not only descriptive but also active, and in its most literal sense, creative. Language has the ability to create the realities in which we live. The common example of this phenomenon is the phrase "I do." In certain contexts, as a response to a question, it might not have any more significance than a simple answer. But within the context of a wedding, saying "I do" literally *does something*: it marks the moment when the couple is announced married, serving as not only a vocal annunciation but also a romantic and legal bond.

Communicating is a design activity. On a surface level, we are literally designing a conversation. In a deeper sense, linguistic communication is an *attempt* to convey a particular message or create a particular outcome, similar to design as an attempt to communicate preferred uses or ways to solve a problem. In this sense, language is not always about communicating a sense of truth but rather is concerned with fitting into an appropriate context. Speaking of truth might be the end goal of something like hard scientific research, and thus fits within the context of a lab setting, but is mostly foreign to everyday conversation. Similarly, walking into a scientific research lab and announcing "I do" would be quite strange. So when we make sense of designed objects and communicate that sense to a wider audience, its transfer into meaning systems is dependent on whether the communication of sense fits the context of others in the network. As mentioned before, experience designers are by and large very aware of the importance of context in communication. The problem is that understanding contextual systems is difficult and time consuming. It calls for a very deep understanding of thinking and behavior, often beyond what clients are willing to finance. The point here is not to shame designers but rather to emphasize the idea that the designs created and released into the world are not simply descriptive—they are creating new realities.

This need to account for communicative contexts necessitates a mediation between communication and usability. We might think of a piece of artwork as an object designed (mostly) without constraints. It is, in a sense, pure declaration without usability. Designed objects, on the other hand, must be usable. The question, therefore, becomes to what extent the designer is concerned with either one:

> The designer is not so much called upon to make functions visible as to make things ready-to-hand and so transform things into tools. The paradigm of expression can also be criticized, because it fails to recognize the character of design as declarative act. In its ontological structure design is related to declarative statements. This type of statement does not depict anything, it does not describe anything; rather, it produces a reality, as when a chairman says he declares a meeting open or ended. The statement that a form expresses a function is not a description of an objective fact, it is the declaration that a certain object is there for a purpose, for instance to be sat upon. Of course, that is not an arbitrary act, since the declaration is made by members of a language community, with its own standard practices. These practices say that the in-order-to of chairs is not a surface to write upon and they are not fuel to be burnt.[181]

This mix of declarative/creative and usable is a crucial goal for designers. It allows designers to consider the dual role of considering use contexts and creating affordances to enable use, all while promoting individual sensemaking and systemic meaning.

How to make this usable/communicative/sensical/meaningful experience happen is a different question. Each design project has its unique challenges, of course. But a commonality among designed objects is the interface. Beyond common conceptions of interfaces as digital screens, we need to think about the interface broadly as the point at which user and object come together—the point that enables use. In the next chapter, we'll attempt to better understand the interface as a point of contact and communication of usability and meaning.

Interface

If we accept Krippendorff's distinction between meaning and sense, we can assert that the interface is the point of sensemaking between user and object and context. Krippendorff holds that sensemaking is essentially an individual act between user and object. We cannot make sense of things by simply considering them from afar as scientific or present-at-hand objects. Instead, sense comes from the active use of the object, and the interface serves to facilitate this use. The interface, then, is the point at which use and sense occur. The remainder of this section will focus on trying to extrapolate what an interface is, how it functions, and how it mediates object use.

We'll begin with the various definitions and accounts of the interface. At ground level, the word "inter-face" is quite literal in its significance. "Inter" is easy enough: between. "Face" is a bit more complicated, as it can point to "face" in the sense of that which allows communication between two humans. People in conversation focus on the face of the other, taking cues from expressions and various contortions of the facial muscles, to the nodding or shaking of the head in response. "Face" is also how we recognize others. More so than other parts of the body, we remember faces as points of recognition and emotional attachment to one another. A preliminary definition of an interface, then, might be: that which enables communication, interaction, and recognition between two separate entities. But, of course, this definition is insufficient.

Beginning with less of a definition and more of a statement, Bonsiepe says that "without interface there are no tools."[182] If we are to accept the preliminary definition provided above, the interface becomes the point of structural coupling between human and object through which all use is enabled. Bonsiepe adds to this definition by asserting that the interface is necessary for what we know as tools, or objects that have a discrete purpose and are used to accomplish goals. The interface, for Bonsiepe, is an essential part of this interaction, as it enables the structural coupling necessary to use a tool seamlessly, and to enable the readiness-to-hand that causes the object (and the interface) to fade into the background of the experience. On the other hand, we can think of the interface as "an 'agitation' or generative friction between different formats."[183] In addition to a gateway into seamlessness, the interface is also a point of contention between two different things or modes of being—not necessarily the inner and outer, but simply two different things. As the point of structural coupling, the interface is always fitting two things together that do not "naturally" fit. There is an artificial coupling, which will always cause some form of tension.

In a certain sense, the interface is a concentration of affordances, or the place where primary and secondary affordances communicate action. In the case of the water bottle, we might think of the primary interface as the spout: it is what allows the bottle to perform its primary function. Other affordances such as the cap, threading on the spout that allow the user to close the bottle, or ridges on the side that allow the user to grip the bottle are secondary in the sense that "closing" and "holding" support the end goal of "drinking" or "quenching thirst," but are not necessary to that end goal. The interface changes based on perspective and end goal. After drinking, the primary interface shifts from the spout to the cap and threading, as the primary goal has shifted from drinking to closing. So what we determine as the interface is always contextual to the end goal, which of course is always moving. Just like the movement between ready-to-hand and present-at-hand, or embodied relations to hermeneutic, the relationship between interface, affordance, and goal is in a constant state of movement.

Bonsiepe identifies the interface as the central focus for designers:

The interface is the central domain on which the designer focuses attention. The design of the interface determines the scope for action by the user of products. The interface reveals the character of objects as tools and the information contained in data. It makes objects into products, it makes data into comprehensible information and—to use Heidegger's terminology—it makes ready-to-hand *(Zuhandenheit)* as opposed to present-at-hand *(Vorhandenheit)*.[184]

I find this view quite limiting. While I agree on the overall notion of the importance of the interface, I do not believe we can accurately say that the interface is "the central domain" for designers' attention. This view focuses on the physical object of design and forgets about the role of user behaviors, and all the variability the goes along with it. If affordances and interfaces are shifting according to users' goals, then of course designers need to consider behavioral patters beyond the interface one is currently designing. The interface will be heavily influenced by those behavioral observations. It also ignores everything that comes after the interface is designed—how it is used, if it is effective, etc. Both of these concerns are of central focus for designers, as well. This points to a larger concern, especially within experience design, that deals with the fetishization of the interface. Designers working in market-driven contexts tend to present the interface as *the* object of design work for their clients. Clients, on the other end, become accustomed to receiving tangible results for the budgets they offer, continuing the cycle on the next project by focusing on what deliverables will be offered instead of approach, principles, methods, etc.

Much of this problem goes back to the fundamental error of assuming an inherent and observable difference between the internal and external, mind and body. According to this dualist tendency, we can see the interface as the connective tissue between inner and outer, and thus presenting the interface design as the most important part of the design process allows us to believe the illusion that we are becoming better connected to the "external" world. It becomes the tangible thing for which clients exchange their money. And while this approach has certainly been lucrative for many design firms, it is coming back around to create an atmosphere of repetitive labor. Herbert Simon famously articulated his idea of an artifact as "a meeting point, an 'interface' in today's terms between an 'inner' environment, the substance and organization of the artifact itself, and an 'outer' environment, the surroundings in which it operates."[185] For Simon, artifacts are all about the ability to serve a purpose, and designer intention is highly important to the "success" of an artifact. His attempt to describe design as a scientific process lead to statements such as "If the inner environment is appropriate to the outer environment, or vice versa, the artifact will serve its intended purpose." It is not difficult to see how the post-phenomenological framework presented in this book would take issue with a positivist statement like this. When experience designers present their work in the form of an interface design, the implicit promise is that "this is our idea for how to bridge the inner and outer.." And, when presented in such a way, clients can easily slip into believing that the interface is a reliable mode of intentional mediation, somehow resulting in stronger customer-business interface and more sales.

These conceptions of the interface have their problems, but they serve as points of examination for the deeper issues within interface theory and experience design practice. Moving to some more recent examinations, Branden Hookway provides one of the most comprehensive definitions:

> A preliminary definition of interface is as follows: the interface is a form of relation that obtains between two or more distinct entities, conditions, or states such that it only comes into being as these distinct entities enter into an active relation with one another; such that it actively maintains, polices, and draws on the separation that renders these entities as distinct at the same time as it selectively allows transmission or communication of force or information from one entity to another; and such that its overall activity brings about the production of a united condition or system that is mutually defined through the regulated and specified interrelations of these distinct entities. [...] The interface is defined in its coupling of the processes of holding apart and drawing together, of confining and opening up, of disciplining and enabling, of excluding and including.[186]

Here, we see the previously mentioned definitions come together. Hookway describes the interface in terms of the constant movement—the drawing together and pulling apart of two sides. It begins as "two distinct entities enter into an active relation with one another," for which we might think of a user and system as these distinct entities, despite the argument to be made that users and the systems with which they interact might not be completely separate. Given the bringing-together of what was once separate, the interface is a point of tension between these two different forces. It both "actively maintains, polices, and draws on the separation" but still "selectively allows transmission or communication." The interface is perpetually moving between similarity and difference—it mediates the vast differences between user and system, for example, while still allowing for the communication of certain information from one side in a way that the other understands. Finally, the mediation function of the interface results in emergent systems or a "united condition" that partially merges its two sides. We might think of this as a third entity: user, system, and user-system. The interface, then, is not a passive connection but rather an active mediation point that brings together different modes.

As technology increased in complexity during the Industrial Revolution and approaching the digital age, the interface became what Krippendorff[187] called "prototypical artifact of the postindustrial era."

Perhaps especially as computers became "personal" computers, the interface became the focal object for much of design work attempting to bridge the gap between users and these complex machines, and thus translate the complexity of computing for non-technical users. As a result, the user-system entity came into the forefront. The interface might be a point of tension, as we saw earlier, but the era of personal computing has gone to great lengths to minimize the user's consciousness of that tension. "An important property of interfaces is that they weave human sensory–motor coordination and an artifact's reactivity into a dynamic whole that human participants in the interface can understand and feel comfortable being in. The human body is as much part of an interface as the artifact interacted with."[188] Digital designers aim to make users feel at home within the interface, incorporating the body when possible. Of course, the most obvious examples are gestural and the other so-called "natural" user interfaces—as they rely more heavily on direct manipulation of content as opposed to representations and metaphor—ostensibly creating a more natural way of interacting through the interface. The overarching goal of consumer-facing interface design came to instill a sense of familiarity and ease within the interactive space.

The instinct for many designers is to apply familiar terms of "intuition" and "invisibility" to descriptions of optimal interface designs. These descriptors are turning into catch-all words meant to explain other qualities such as ease of use, smooth interaction, and noninvasiveness. As I have argued elsewhere,[189] these adjectives are inaccurate and potentially harmful. Analogies such as intuition and invisibility are mundane but harmful. They are often used to explain to clients or non-design audiences that interfaces will be easy to use, without requiring any special instruction, and in fact so easy that the user will forget they are there. Harking back to discussions of readiness-to-hand, we can see how this view is attractive and in a certain sense appropriate to a phenomenological conception of the interface. The problem is that these descriptors become overused and work themselves into the practical discourse of design, causing professional designers to take their implications for granted and over-simplify their own work. Calling an interface "intuitive," or striving to design an interface that is invisible, takes the "unsemiotic" nature of affordances very seriously, perhaps too seriously. The implicit goal is to create an interface that communicates its affordances in the clearest, most "natural," and most non-conscious manner as possible, so that a user might automatically know how to use the interface without calling upon cultural, linguistic, or learned information. The problem is that almost all of our interactions call upon this type of information, and design principles that call for its eradication are almost impossible to achieve.

After all, designers are in the business of creating the artificial. We can certainly create objects that attempt to communicate their use, but this attempt is just that: an attempt. The use of prototypes and frequent testing is of great importance given these design goals around invisibility and intuition; it is not an easy, cheap, or quick process to achieve this type of outcome. And in many cases, this radically smooth interaction is not at all desirable. We might want to highlight the interface or the object of design as an object in order to sustain conscious awareness. Even if the advocate is unaware, arguments for intuition and invisibility often insert a hierarchical relationship between smooth interaction and conscious interaction, assuming the former is always desirable to the latter. One might even use Heidegger's conception of presence-at-hand and readiness-to-hand as the basis for the argument, forgetting or ignoring the sense that Heidegger did not necessarily advocate one as *better* than the other. He was merely articulating readiness-to-hand as a more common mode of interaction.

> From a postphenomenological perspective, the interface needs not always become transparent to be useful for people. [...] A designer striving to perfect the embodied relation between a guide dog and its user may well devise a new leash that improves maneuverability without drawing much attention to it. However, in the case of the alterity relation identified, a designer could change the uniform of the skiing instructor to highlight his bodily demonstration. In the latter example, making the instructor's body stand out more (and thus be less 'transparent') may facilitate the learning of skills by beginning students and sustain the fantasy that they will soon move as effortlessly as the instructor.[190]

The use of the word "transparency" here is important. A transparent object is quite different from an invisible one. Invisibility implies a complete lack of awareness in everyday situations, and the inability to come into consciousness without some kind of mediating factor. Take microscopic life forms, for example. We know they exist, even though we cannot perceive them without a microscope. They are invisible—we cannot interact with them on a conscious level without the aid of something else.

A transparent object, however, is something we *perceive through*, such as a window. We can infer its existence due to the lack of a draft or if we touch it, but looking though it does not imply its existence. The big difference here between the transparent and the invisible is that we can bring the former into awareness without the aid of other influences. The object is free to move in and out of conscious awareness; back and forth between the foreground and background of perception. I would argue that transparency is a much more attainable and preferable design goal than invisibility because it allows for this type of movement.

Michael May connects the ideas of intuition and affordances by explaining design's latching onto affordance according to the following logic: "If animals rely on direct perception of affordances as they move around in their natural environments, we as humans should be able to use artifacts of our cultural environment by relying on the designed affordances of the technology, e.g. from the handle on the coffee cup to the remote control for the TV."[191] But this view becomes problematic when we consider that "in any actual social and cultural context of use, artifacts will acquire additional meaning from the network of relations and actions they are involved in, and from the discourses regulating and articulating these activities."[192] Affordances certainly do point to intuition, but it is unclear that any human interaction can be free of cultural/artificial influence. Meaning systems pervade every aspect of existence. The intuition argument also implies that there is some kind of transcendent meaning one can embed into a design. Yet, if we accept Krippendorff's claim that use is necessary for sensemaking, then communicating this transcendent meaning upon initial perception becomes increasingly difficult.

Much of the anxiety around product development in market-driven contexts stems from client communication. Designers need to assure their clients that what they create will be easy to use—a deceptively complex phrase with multiple facets and influences. Invisibility and intuition are convenient, mundane, and easily understandable descriptors designers can use to assure clients of the product's eventual success. The quest for perfection is an invasive one. Perhaps a more accurate, and certainly more difficult, way of explaining the potential future success of a product is through the lens of coping we covered in chapter 2. Humans are highly adaptable, and the phenomenological account of everyday Dasein is one of coping—finding ways to adapt to various environmental influences. More contemporary experience design methods are beginning to account for this variability—again through rapid prototyping and continuous testing—but it is far from a rigorous process at the moment.

Methods are one side of the potential solution, but a reframing of client communication is also necessary. Clients paying large sums of money certainly do not want to hear about variability, multistability, and adaptability, so it is necessary to introduce these ideas delicately. Phenomenology can help achieve this through a shift in language from invisibility to transparency, explaining that "transparency enables people to sustain their *relationship* with the product, even when something goes wrong."[193] Instead of an "invisible" interface that breaks and might be forgotten, the transparent interface continues to remain conscious so the user can deal with it and work around its shortcomings if necessary.

> Transparency of use embodies an experiential form of the distinction between transparency and opacity. Transparency here is a form of perceptual 'neutrality'; technologies function as a perspicuous interface between humans and world. Transparency of context, in addition to this, embodies a more cognitive dimension of the distinction; it concerns our awareness of the mediating role technologies play rather than our direct experience of the technologies themselves.[194]

With transparency, we can more closely examine the mediating role that technology, especially the interface, plays in everyday interaction. The transparent interface is not completely invisible, but it is also not invasive. The user senses its presence without feeling unnecessarily burdened by it. Transparency is neither active nor passive, neither exhibitionistic nor voyeuristic.

Don Ihde explains a strange paradox in this desire for invisibility as it relates to his own theory of embodied relations:

> There is also a deeper desire which can arise from the experience of embodiment relations. It is the doubled desire that, on one side, is a wish for *total transparency*, total embodiment, for the technology to truly 'become me.' Were this possible, it would be equivalent to there being no technology, for total transparency would *be* my body and senses; I desire the face-to-face that I would experience without the technology. But that is only one side of the desire. The other side is the desire to have the power, the transformation that

the technology makes available. Only by using the technology is my bodily power enhanced and magnified by speed, through distance, or by any of the other ways in which technologies change my capacities. These capacities are always *different* from my naked capabilities. The desire is, at best, contradictory. I want the transformation that the technology allows, but I want it in such a way that I am basically unaware of its presence. I want it in such a way that it becomes me.[195]

Embedded within the call for invisible interfaces is its logical conclusion of complete bodily and cognitive incorporation. Visions of the Borg are abundant here, and for good reason. This desire for invisibility is related to work involved with interaction: assuming that users desire a "seamless" experience points to the idea that interaction is difficult, and that decreasing the workload of interaction is preferable. With this in mind, we can see how Heidegger's fears of humans assuming a passive position over and against technology might not have been so paranoid. The conclusion of decreasing the labor of interaction is a docile state in which technology—if we can accept that technology acts and evolves as a result of larger meaning systems—could actually embed itself into Dasein.

The story of the kettle accident in the previous chapter is again relevant here. The interfaces of the handle and spout came to be invisible, resulting in physical harm. Their multistability caused the spout to become no longer a spout, but a tool to scratch. If designers are unable to dictate how affordances communicate, then the question becomes how to design for the most beneficial outcomes, whether a singular outcome or many. We now turn to recent applications of embodiment to the design process, and to a theory of design in general in order to begin thinking about a way of responsibly designing less invasive interfaces.

Embodied Design Practice

Chapter 4 focused on the dualisms found within design practices, with the promise of returning to them at some point. The goal for the remainder of this book is to begin sketching out what these embodied, non-dualist design methods influenced by phenomenology might look like. In this section, we will remain focused on the idea of embodiment in the design process, as opposed to a more rationalist, Cartesian methodology. And in the next chapter, we will shift to a specifically phenomenological method of experience design.

The human-centered process advocated by design thinking in general is particularly well-suited to embodied design practice. What this movement accomplished is a consideration for end users as an important part of design. Where I think the design community has failed—and where I hope this book can contribute—is a concern for deep understanding of the human experience. So far, we have established that experience is much more complex than the dualist notions introduced by Descartes. The question now is how to apply the phenomenological concepts covered thus far to a new perspective on experience design. Beginning with the human-centered movement and its offshoots—namely Krippendorff's "semantic turn"—we can show how care and concern, in the phenomenological senses of the words, for embodied experience can enhance what experience designers have built so far:

> This is a move from the image of humans as having to adapt to technological progress and of designers as making adaptation less painful, to the image of humans as able to influence the direction of technological development and of designers as finding ways to support diverse practices of living, community, and the sense needed for individuals to feel at home. It is a move toward human-centeredness, the acknowledgement that meaning matters. This is the core of the semantic turn.[196]

The semantic turn begins with human-centeredness and continues with the need to consider semantics, or how designs communicate. It is a movement from pure usability, or the need to make the inconveniences of everyday life less frustrating, to an extended consideration for imagining new ways of being in the world that radically rethinks the current state of existence. "The willingness to imagine worlds in which humans feel at home and initiate collective efforts to realize them for the benefit of everyone who cares is a mark of a postindustrial society. It makes design the driving activity of the postindustrial society. [...] [D]esign has shifted from being product- or production-centered to a human-centered effort."[197] The semantic turn extends even beyond human-centricity into the desire to create new "homes" for end users, or the sense that designers can apply their work further than decreasing frustration, and into the production of more home-like places.

Emerging design practices, such as service design[198] and speculative and critical design,[199] might be viewed as a continuation of the semantic turn to what we might call a "systemic turn" (just to add another "turn" into the mix). These contemporary practices specifically call out the need for systemic thinking, or the complex blend of interfaces and cultural-semiotic systems, problems, and solutions. Discourse in experience design in general is also adopting a systemic view of design more than ever before. Whether designers are practicing what they advocate is another question, but it would be difficult to find an experience designer who encourages narrow, interface-level thinking over systems thinking. The systemic turn has to do with systems, but it also concerns a consciousness of places within that system. In other words, systemic design methods are able to zoom in and out based on need, moving from macro-views of service ecologies to micro-views of product interfaces. Systemic approaches account for both the advantages of a macro view and the situated-ness of humans within the system.

As a design practice specifically interested in systems, service design is becoming increasingly difficult to distinguish from experience design. For our purposes, we might say that product design focuses on individual products in a system, service design focuses on how products interact with humans to form a system, and experience design focuses on the *experience of* that system. There is significant overlap, of course, but it is useful make these distinctions. Both service design and experience design deal with systems in different ways. Service design will look at how context or situated-ness relates to crafting service ecosystems in which actants (to use a term from actor-network theory) attempt to accomplish their goals. Experience design might do the same, but from a slightly different angle—that of the individual experience. With both approaches, the role of situated design is highly important. "Rather than a conservative account of design that sees design solely as a problem solving activity, a situated approach to design, where understanding or construction of the situation is core, emphasises creative research into the situated nature of the problem space, with theories deriving from design investigation as much as contributing to it."[200] Situated design methods go beyond a more sterile version of problem solving, and into the complex systems of experience. Instead of "solving problem *a* with solution *b,*" it moves into the complex spaces of interaction to determine multiple potential solutions to a constantly shifting problem space. The "conservative" account Brereton mentions—the pure problem solving model of design—runs on many assumptions pointed out in chapters 3 and 4, one of which is that we cannot design based on simple equations, as the act of "solutioning" will almost always result in a new perspective on the problem space. Situated design methods account for the idea that "context isn't just 'there,' but is actively produced, maintained and enacted in the course of the activity at hand."[201]

Dourish's work on the notion of context and what it means for computing is particularly relevant here. In addition to articulating a theory of context based on embodied cognition, he extended his thinking into areas of design with what he called embodied interaction. This concept of embodied interaction is not necessarily limited to interaction design as we know it today, but rather Dourish was getting at a larger theory of interaction that we can now apply to design practices. It is probably no surprise that ethnography is a key method for embodied interaction and situated design, given its concern with in-context probing and adaptability to change.

> [Ethnographers] give us ways of approaching design. Still, they typically go beyond specific instances of design. More to the point, they draw in general on the fundamental repudiation of a traditional separation between designer and user, between technology and practice. To the extent that these implications are not formulated as implications for design, it is because the categories of design, user, and designer are themselves in question.[202]

Ethnographic methods provide insight into systems of meaning that blend categories commonly separated by design. Somewhat similar to actor-network theory and its attention to human and non-human actants, ethnography, at least in its anthropological form, tends to not separate designers from users but rather views them within the same system. That is not to say designers and users have no distinguishing characteristics, but rather that the overlap is so significant in everyday life that it does not warrant hard categorization. Ethnography, in its purest form, does not necessarily have direct implications for design, focusing instead on the cultural and meaning systems of everyday life. From there, designers might step in and interpret these findings through a designer-ly lens in order to extract useful insights in design practice. Researchers might also apply more focused methods from "design ethnography," which tends to use traditional ethnography with a greater concern for specific design problems.

The main concern for embodied interaction and design ethnography is, of course, the role of context. It serves as a framework for understanding the emergent properties of interaction—the idea that designer intention and purposeful design cannot dictate the emergence of new variables in an interactive system. "The essential feature of embodied interaction is the idea [...] of allowing users to negotiate and evolve systems of practice and meaning in the course of their interaction with information systems."[203] Embodied interaction gives designers the building blocks to embrace the uncertainty of multistable technologies. It also calls for a deep care, in the Heideggerian sense, for embodiment as what constitutes interaction: "What I am claiming for 'embodied interaction' is not simply that it is a form of interaction that is embodied, but rather that it is an approach to the design and analysis of interaction that takes embodiment to be central to, even constitutive of, the whole phenomenon."[204] But before designers get to this level of care, it is necessary to shed the Cartesian and positivist baggage mentioned throughout this book, and in turn begin to articulate a theory of design thinking informed by phenomenological philosophy.

Chapter 7
Concluding Remarks

Phenomenological Design Thinking

"To apply a phenomenological approach to design is to focus at the dual question of how design, as a medium of meaning formation, both relates to and possibly changes the constituents of experience."[205]

Given that the tone I set out at the beginning is somewhere between academia and practice—and thus calling out the fundamental flaw with that dichotomy—I feel the onus is on me to make the more "theoretical" aspects of the text more applicable to design practice. This does not mean, however, that a strict methodology or set of practices is needed: I have little interest, at least right now, in packaging a design practice influenced by phenomenology and associated theory into an "off-the-shelf" set of practices. Instead, it is more productive at this point to re-examine some existing methods through the lens of phenomenology and take some of the key points of this book to apply them, perhaps more than I have done so far, to design practices.

Mads Folkmann set up the challenge of phenomenological design thinking quite well in the quote above when he calls for an understanding of both the present and future of experience. Phenomenology and its intellectual cousins are excellent frameworks for thinking about the inductive and abductive aspects of design. If design is truly unique in its ability to push thinking toward future scenarios, then present experience is certainly an important aspect of that. It turns out that a theory of phenomenological design thinking is not terribly different from post-phenomenology as we have already discussed—it is simply an evolution. In its focus on things and the nature of interaction, post-phenomenology has already begun to push classical phenomenological thinking into the realm of design. It is my view that the next step in post-phenomenology is grounded in design thinking. The remainder of this final chapter will be spent revisiting some concepts already mentioned with a particular focus on design practices.

Praxis

Hopefully this book has served to showcase the importance of praxis: theory-informed practice, or the idea of a cyclical relationship between theory and practice, for which the practical process is as of tantamount importance as its end result. I mentioned in the introduction that the book is neither theoretical nor practical, but both; neither academic nor industry-focused, but both. It should be no surprise that I see these dichotomies of academia/industry and theory/practice as detrimental. Especially in design, where we at least claim to be a multidisciplinary field, these walls we put up are completely counterintuitive. While academia and industry might have different end goals—the production of knowledge versus commercial success—these goals are wrapped up within one another. The production of knowledge and commercial success are not mutually exclusive, as much as many purists on both sides like to believe. There is nothing inherently wrong with achieving commercial success built on academic knowledge, and using commercial design to inform future academic research ensures that research is grounded in worldly practice.

We have seen how phenomenology posits praxis as our way of being in the world. It is anti-dualist in the sense that it rejects the Cartesian separation of mind and body, thus integrating self and world into Dasein. Dasein's focus on being-in, as in being-involved, as a conglomeration of self and world that exhibits care and concern over itself as Dasein translates over to how Dasein makes use of designed objects. It is with great care that humans interact with their world, and designers must always work around that care.

Many design practices and outputs, I believe, are aimed at recognizing praxis and designing for care, but most begin to fragment under the weight of commercial clients or academic pressures. Take user personas for example. Personas play an excellent role in summarizing research results to be spread through an organization with little need to dig into raw data. They give design teams a personal identification to users and a set of characteristics to focus on while designing. However, all the benefits of personas do not counterbalance their inherent decontextualization. A persona does not experience anything—humans do. So even as a helpful document within the design process, it also reinforces the problematic dualism left over from Descartes. Personas represent detached understanding; even when based on the most rigorous research methods, they are theoretical formulations.

The point here is not to suggest new design practices to replace these old ones, but rather to simply point out their limitations. The onus is on designers to recognize these limitations and to avoid using these methods beyond their capabilities. The ways designers frame their practices make all the difference.

Primacy of Things

As we have seen throughout this book, things are our means to knowledge and understanding. Interaction with things, not only as "other" objects but also as embodied means of accomplishment, frames our entire experience of the world and allows for hermeneutic interpretation of everyday life. Understanding systems of things and how humans experience them is the domain of experience design.

The complexity of this statement lies in the idea that experience design deals with both the tangible and intangible. It is the design of experience, which implies that we must also design the things that are experienced. Experience design always has an object; it is the experience designer who crafts the experience of products and services by ensuring an understanding of things and meaning systems. The designer is concerned with both systems and things, attempting to create the conditions of possibility for intended results, and to craft clear affordances and play with the movement from embodiment to external.

Thinking back to Heidegger's modes of interaction—the present-at-hand and ready-to-hand—I made the point that these are not necessarily exclusive categories but rather a continuum of interaction. Interactions are almost always in some state of movement back and forth between these categories. Simply typing on a keyboard is a constant state of embodied, ready-to-hand interaction that can be interrupted by a mis-typed letter, second-guessing oneself about the spelling of a word, or distractions in the environment. In this way, it is much too simplistic to state invisibility, intuition, or readiness-to-hand as a design goal. They are not distinct categories but simply different modes of interaction, only judged as "good" or "bad" according to the context of use. It is the same with Don Ihde's four categories: embodied, hermeneutic, alterity, and background. There is nothing qualitatively better about a background relation and an embodied relation. We cannot make the mistake of believing an "intuitive" interface is always good. It is up to experience designers, as the makers of experiential systems, to determine the use contexts and narrative points at which we might apply different interaction styles.

Multistability

We have established that the human-technology relationship is multistable, and this inherent variability and adaptability can be difficult for designers to incorporate into their work. Especially when working with commercial clients, there is an impulse to portray as much certainty as possible. Clients are paying large sums of money for a design team to plan and execute—the last thing that team wants to do is give any impression that the clients money might not produce the desired results, or that users might interpret design intentions in an unanticipated way. The design team, then, meticulously plans their process, executes, and attempts to measure results in a way that confirm their original intentions.

Multistability is the force that makes all this pantomime for nothing. Designs will almost always be adapted from the original designer intention. The powers of creative misuse will always win against the clearest affordances and easiest paths to completion. When we think about experience design, methods such as usability testing cease to be about creating perfection or removing "un-intuitive" features, and instead about observing coping strategies. The ways that users cope with problems are the core insights for usability and future design.

The Problem-Solution Paradox

Of all the paradoxes found within design, the paradox of problems and solutions probably has the most impact. Stretching across design disciplines and practices, we can see its effects on almost any given design project. It is the hermeneutic circle of design. The parts are inherently connected to the whole, and the whole to its parts. This paradox creates massive problems, especially on commercial design projects where clients desire a deep and unflinching knowledge of a "process," and designers are forced to deliver this illusory knowledge knowing that it is insufficient. The paradox calls for a certain amount of play—a fluid movement from problem definition to solution exploration, and back. This, of course, causes ambiguity in project plans and billing cycles.

It is evident that experience design needs better ways to account for the paradox and create plans that are flexible enough for forward and backward movement between problem and solution exploration. Criticism against waterfall product development usually revolves around its hyper-linearity and its tendency to establish rigid phases with little room for error. Essentially, waterfall ignores that the design process is full of error and variability, and that designers are quite suited for adapting to such unexpected outcomes. Waterfall assumes a positivist version of the design process: we gather knowledge, formulate a plan based on that knowledge, and then execute it. Much like the Cartesian separation of mind and body, along with the emphasis on intentional action, waterfall design relies on the intentional process of planning to drive execution, leaving almost no opportunity to adapt. I hope this book has shown that experience design, like any other practice, involves an embodied, situated movement between present and future states. Phenomenology and its offshoots can help us better understand how design-as-praxis takes shape, and how it might affect how designers design.

Care

One of the biggest tensions in experience design involves the question of skillful practice. As practitioners continue to add more diverse skills, what exactly constitutes an "experience designer" is only becoming more ambiguous. For an industry that prides itself on creating clear, meaningful, and useful systems, experience design has ironically done a terrible job of applying those goals to define itself as a design discipline—the cobbler's children, I suppose. Design practices cluster together and strip apart so quickly that we can hardly make sense of them, resulting in trivial arguments over whether experience designers should be able to code, and training programs teaching experience design as if it were a trade. What we have lost sight of in this process is the care and responsibility involved in designing experience.

Design is an un-throwing, as Henk Oosterling describes it. Humans design to take an active part in their world; to shape an experience instead of remaining content with our current situation. We call a designer a "designer" because of the care they exhibit toward materials, users, objects, experiences, etc. As experience designers incorporate more practices, and we see individuals taking on more and more aspects of the design process, I fear that care is eroded as it spreads thinly across various concerns. For projects with any kind of complexity, we need to maintain a certain amount of specialization on a design team. We need people to focus and avoid switching styles of thinking too rapidly. While the division of labor in experience design might not always be financially advantageous, it allows for a deeper sense of concern for a limited, manageable set of practices.

Practice

One might read this book as looking toward a phenomenological design process—and in some respects it is—but nothing discussed in this book is revolutionary. It is composed of existing theory applied to new contexts. The value of phenomenological thinking is obviously not limited to design, and, I might argue, is so wide-ranging that it becomes difficult if not impossible to pin down to one area. Nonetheless, what phenomenology accomplishes for design is it establishes bases of knowledge around experience. Instead of completely new practices, phenomenological theory helps explain current practices, add to them, and perhaps make them a bit more rigorous. Design is inherently phenomenological, so forcing new practices at this point does not seem particularly beneficial.

Perhaps the most useful peculiarity design offers is its ability to push into the future. Plenty of intellectual efforts exist to determine a sense of truth about the past. Insofar as the present essentially doesn't exist—for example, is "now" when I utter the word, or when its meaning is interpreted?—the acts of inductive and deductive reasoning work to establish explanations of what we currently experience. Design, as we have seen, uses that knowledge to extend into future experiences via the abductive gesture. Analytical and creative thinking come together with equal importance to create a holistic view of design; we cannot effectively create the future without knowing the past, and we cannot completely understand the past without envisioning the future. This back-and-forth play between past and future shapes design processes from understanding to visioning to sketching to prototyping to critique and back. These activities contain many movements, the most important of which are familiarization/de-familiarization and concealment/unconcealment. We can think of these as the ends of a spectrum with many points in between. Design practices play in the space between these poles, constantly using this sense of play to elicit new outcomes. Designers bring the familiar close, only to make it strange again. They move from macro- to micro-perspectives on design problems, concealing and unconcealing what is or is not useful at any given time.

This foreground-background movement we see throughout phenomenology is an integral part of design. We see it in Heidegger's present-at-hand and ready-to-hand object relations, in which the interaction with objects moves in and out of our field of consciousness. The object moves from familiar to unfamiliar and back—whether present-at-hand or ready-to-hand corresponds to familiar or unfamiliar depends on perspective. Within experience design, we see this movement of familiarization/defamiliarization and foreground/background in activities such as ethnographic research and structured ideation. Research methods work to validate designers' assumptions about the world by gathering evidence about the applicability of personal biases. The hyper-familiar bias about the world and those in it becomes de-familiarized when we go out into the world and actively observe. I might believe that caregivers for a terminally ill patient, for example, might experience problems with managing the time they devote to a patient and time they devote to work and family. It's a valid assumption to make, but its hyper-familiarity must be disturbed by actual observation and dialogue with real caregivers. This would lead to a de-familiarization of the original assumption, potentially showing it to be invalid, or at least adding some more detail to it. Similarly, once a core problem is observed and designers work to discover potential solutions, their work shifts to concealment and unconcealment, or micro- and macro-level views of a problem space. Diagramming, especially systems and flow diagramming, allows designers to zoom in and out on various aspects of problem and solution spaces. When zoomed into a micro-level view, such as when sketching the screen of a digital interface, the remainder of the system is obscured to the designer's view—this is much like Don Ihde's conception of the telescope allowing the user to see far distances while obscuring what is close by. Similarly, when sketching macro-level systems and flows, it allows for a wide view that obscures the details. Each perspective has its value; the role of design is to determine when one perspective is preferable over the other. The role of the designer includes deciding when to conceal and unconceal, and to recognize the role of familiarization and de-familiarization.

This discussion leads us to a few statements that we can make about experience design from a phenomenological perspective. These statements are not necessarily design principles or heuristics but rather some general statements that should help sum up previous discussions:

1) Humans exist in context

Experience designers would often like to fully consider networks of interaction or context of use, but they lack the necessary tools/budget/time to do so. The default position is to hyperfocus on a small part of the network, which leads to false assumptions. When asked outright, experience designers will almost always say that context matters. We cannot understand users as divorced from the contextual forces that shape their behavior. And yet, our work says something different. The fetishization of deliverables leads to an inauthentic relationship with the work we do. We all know at a gut level that documentation is really just a way to help us think--it serves to communicate decisions. In the end, however, a sketch or a diagram plays the primary role of helping the designer think through a complex situation. Even when done well, these documents are inherently disconnected from use context. They are representations. The point here is not to abandon design methods but rather to call out what they lack. This awareness allows us to use things like user personas and use cases not as deliverables but as ways to facilitate thinking. Creating the document is not the real work; understanding results from thinking through the object provides the real value.

2) Thinking does not always precede action

It is common in experience design to assume—consciously or unconsciously—that thought precedes action. This is the idea that humans formulate theoretical or representational thoughts, and then act on them. Heidegger posits that our behavior is goal-oriented—we use objects in order to accomplish goals. This basic insight frames the bulk of interaction design work. We design systems that aim to hit on key goals and tasks identified as important to users because we understand that people will put a product to use in order to accomplish an end goal. What this approach misses, however, is the potential for new end goals that only emerge after we begin interacting with something. That is, once a product is in use, users might discover new goals of which they were previously unaware, and which the current product might help attain. We can also have negative goals to prevent certain things from happening.

Much of cognitive science and metaphysics assumes that behavior is a result of cognition. Flowing from Cartesian models of the rational being, we have adopted into our collective consciousness the idea that our minds are authoritative entities, serving an executive function to drive behavior. However, recent research in embodied cognition is rethinking the relationship between mind and body from a scientific, as opposed to philosophical, perspective. We now have ways of articulating the idea that our minds are embodied in the world. All this talk of anti-rationality gets us to the concept of praxis, or the act of generating theoretical models through practical outputs. The classic example of learning how to swim, as discussed in chapter 2, is again applied here. When an adult teaches a child to swim, they do not sit down with the child and study fluid dynamics and kinesiology to determine how the body behaves in water. They simply get in the pool. The embodied experience of swimming is much more useful than discrete facts. Only after the experience do we reflect on the experience. This is true of technological experience as well.

3) Intention is not primary

Your intention as a designer is important, but it should not be prioritized over adaptability. So many behaviors are emergent; they only come to be when something new is introduced. Too often, designers assume the role of "designer as deity"—the maker-god who molds the physical world to their image. Perhaps this is why we depict designers in pristine, heavenly environments. Designer intent is important, but it is not the whole story. The "rendering of intent" definition of design is too simplistic to be useful, and it fails to encapsulate the most important parts of design: the embodied use of the designed object and the inherent variability that comes with it. To borrow from post-structuralist thinkers, we might say the designer's intent is irrelevant once the product launches. That is, intent can drive the design process, but that's not the interesting part; the ways in which users adopt the product to their own needs is where the most insight comes from.

Designer intent is a theoretical, speculative formulation, even when based on the most rigorous research methods and valid interpretations. That is not to say intention and strategic positioning are not important, but simply that we need to consider more than idealized outcomes. We need to actually observe use in context. It sounds obvious, but it's not. Technology use is what post-phenomenological thinkers call multistable: its use is not determined by designers but rather has multiple stabilities, or the many use contexts in which its use can take different forms. We can use a car to travel from one place to another. We can also use it as a place to live, a murder weapon, a way to convey social status, or a piece of art. Most often, we are using an object in different ways at different times, and this contextual nature of object use is the most interesting and relevant part for designers. Understanding that context is key to designing, which of course implies that "launch" is not the end of the design process but simply a step toward understanding. Intent only takes us so far. But multistability is not necessarily a wrench in the design machine—it is simply an area of complexity that can sometimes produce serendipitous results.

4) Objects are more than just material

Design is incredibly powerful. It's our responsibility to consider the moral implications of what we design. Post-phenomenologists and other philosophers of technology have focused on this idea heavily in the past decade, especially with the moral/ethical implications of emerging technology. According to Verbeek's theory of mediation discussed earlier, users adopt technological devices as interpretive objects—they are constantly interpreting and rethinking the nature of these things. Objects affect the user as much as the user affects the object. Things like weapons, machines, and even mobile devices have the capacity to mediate the user-world relationship to the point where the user literally changes. Someone in possession of a gun, for example, is very different from someone without one. Bruno Latour's example of the hotel key (from chapter 5) is fitting in that hotel guests no longer make the decision of whether to disobey the sign—the keychain makes the decision for them, which of course calls out the activity of objects. It is easy to get hyper focused on details when caught up in the design process, and forget about the systemic effects an object can have. The things we design have powerful effects on the world, long after the client's check is cashed.

We see the most nefarious effects in things like persuasive design attempting to directly influence behavior—dark patterns attempting to facilitate profitable mistakes—with applications like Secret, which turns your friends into anonymous partners in the confessional booth. But even on a more mundane level, anything we design will have effects that run through the entirety of a product or service ecosystem. Experience designers are not only advocating for users—they are advocating for preferable worlds.

5) Utility does not trump meaning

Client-driven design projects tend to produce an anxiety of perfection. In the real world, nothing works perfectly—we play with things and adapt them to our own needs. When we think about the purposes of usability testing, it is easy to come up reasons related to identifying "unintuitive" interactions, gathering user feedback, fixing any blatant mistakes, and adjusting for more preferable outcomes. While all these points are valid, too many designers approach testing from a point of view that privileges functionality and perfection, ultimately leading to false expectations. The assumption here is that everything we design should work exactly as expected, and functional usability is how we test expectations. Yet, what this approach misses is that 1) Products do not need to be functionally perfect for people to use them. Imperfection will not necessarily cause "abandonment." This language of "abandonment" creates an unnecessary sense of urgency. Humans are remarkably adaptive when value is high and meaning is strong; users are more likely to cope if they experience enough value. 2) Functionality is only half of the story. The interaction between products and users creates meaning, and that is our ultimate concern.

As we saw earlier, Klaus Krippendorff maintains that the goal of product semantics is to identify and optimize opportunities for creating meaning through interaction. What is interesting about Krippendorff's account is that he shifts the conversation from functionality, which can ostensibly be measured with a modicum of what we might call "objectivity," to meaning, which is purely contextual and varies with each individual. It is not terribly difficult to measure functional usability; measuring meaning, however, is a much more delicate and complex process. We know usability standards, and it is relatively easy to communicate them to clients. Meaning, on the other hand, is more slippery and difficult to explain in a way that makes a client want to write you a check. But we should be up to the challenge if we are to move the industry forward. We won't change the multistability of technology, but we can design with it.

In Conclusion

In the introduction, I mentioned that this book suffers from a bit of an identity crisis. On one hand, it is written for experience design practitioners in attempt to show how "theoretical" or "impractical" thinking is necessary for any kind of meaningful design practice, using phenomenological philosophy as one example. Or at the very least, it shows how practitioners can and should engage with the intellectual history of their field beyond self-proclaimed "practical" industry conferences and a few recommended books. On the other hand, this book attempts to balance practitioner focus with depth of analysis; it is interested in establishing a base of knowledge on phenomenological philosophy on which others can build, as opposed to presenting a grand, mostly illusory narrative on how to redefine experience design. Despite the difficulties with identity, I hope that the book has at least provided some perspective on the nature of experience and how we design for it. At the risk of sounding terribly cliché, it is a great time for experience design. Our next move as a budding design discipline is to better understand existing theories of experience while pushing forward into exploring the possibilities they afford. After all, designers are supposed to be good at this type of thing.

About the Author

Thomas Wendt is a New York City based design strategy and research consultant, educator, speaker, and writer.

Client work includes strategic consulting, internal training, and qualitative research projects for companies of all sizes.

Thomas frequently teaches, writes, and speaks on a variety of topics including philosophy and design, information architecture, lean process and theory, design research, and design thinking.

Presentations have been delivered at domestic and international conferences, and his articles have been published in both academic journals and practitioner publications.

Website: srsg.co
Twitter: @thomas_wendt

Bibliography

Agosta, Lou. "A Heideggerian Approach to Empathy." Existenz. 6.2 (2011)

Andler, Daniel. "Context and background. Dreyfus and cognitive science. "Heidegger, coping, and cognitive science 2 (2000): 137.

Austin, John Langshaw. How to do things with words. Vol. 1955. Oxford university press, 1975.

Barthes, Roland. From work to text. 1971.

Basalla, George, ed. The evolution of technology. Cambridge University Press, 1988.

Baudrillard, Jean. "The System of Objects, trans. J. Benedict." London and New York: Verso (1996)

Beckett, Samuel. Three Novels: Molloy, Malone Dies, The Unnamable. New York: Grove, 1995.

Bonsiepe, Gui. Interface: An Approach to Design: in Memoriam Jovita (1941-1998). Jan van Eyck Akademie, Departament of Design, 1999.

Boradkar, Prasad. Designing things: a critical introduction to the culture of objects. Berg Publishers, 2010.

Brereton, Margot, et al. "Reframing the design of context-aware computing." Proceedings of the 25th BCS Conference on Human-Computer Interaction. British Computer Society, 2011.

Brey, Philip. "The social agency of technological artifacts." User Behavior and Technology Development. Springer Netherlands, 2006. 71-80.

Brown, Bill. "Thing theory." Critical Inquiry 28.1 (2001): 1-22.

Brown, Tim. Change by design. HarperCollins, 2009.

Buchanan, Richard. "Wicked problems in design thinking." Design issues (1992): 5-21.

Buchanan, Richard. "Rhetoric, humanism, and design." Discovering design: Explorations in design studies (1995): 23-66.

Chemero, Anthony. Radical embodied cognitive science. MIT press, 2011.

Clark, Andy. Being there: Putting brain, body, and world together again. MIT press, 1997.

Clark, Andy. Supersizing the Mind: Embodiment, Action, and Cognitive Extension: Embodiment, Action, and Cognitive Extension. Oxford University Press, 2008.

Cross, Nigel. Designerly ways of knowing. Springer London, 2006.

Cross, Nigel. Design thinking: Understanding how designers think and work. Berg, 2011.

Derrida, Jacques. "Geschlecht II: Heidegger's hand." Deconstruction and philosophy: The texts of Jacques Derrida 161 (1987): 96.

Descartes, René, and Donald A. Cress. Discourse on method. Hackett Publishing, 1998.

Dorst, Kees, and Nigel Cross. "Creativity in the design process: co-evolution of problem–solution." Design studies 22.5 (2001): 425-437.

Dorst, Kees. "Design problems and design paradoxes." Design issues 22.3 (2006): 4-17.

Dourish, Paul. "Seeking a foundation for context-aware computing." Human–Computer Interaction 16.2-4 (2001): 229-241.

Dourish, Paul. Where the action is: the foundations of embodied interaction. The MIT Press, 2004.

Dourish, Paul, and Genevieve Bell. Divining a digital future: Mess and mythology in ubiquitous computing. Mit Press, 2011.

Dourish, Paul, and Genevieve Bell. "Resistance is futile: reading science fiction alongside ubiquitous computing." Personal and Ubiquitous Computing 18.4 (2014): 769-778.

Dreyfus, Hubert L. Being-in-the-world: A commentary on Heidegger's Being and Time, Division I. The MIT Press, 1991.

Dreyfus, Hubert L. What computers still can't do: a critique of artificial reason. MIT press, 1992.

Dreyfus, Hubert L. "Why Heideggerian AI failed and how fixing it would require making it more Heideggerian." Philosophical psychology 20.2 (2007): 247-268.

Dunne, Anthony, and Fiona Raby. Speculative Everything: Design, Fiction, and Social Dreaming. MIT Press, 2013.

Feenberg, Andrew. "Critical evaluation of Heidegger and Borgmann."Philosophy of Technology: The Technological Condition–An Anthology, Oxford, Blackwell Publishing (2003): 327-337.

Flusser, Vilém. Shape of Things: A Philosophy of Design. Reaktion Books, 2013.

Folkmann, Mads Nygaard. The Aesthetics of Imagination in Design. MIT Press, 2013.

Folkmann, Mads Nygaard. "Agency, Context and Meaning: The Humanities and Design." DRS 2014.

Foucault, Michel. "What is an author." Paul Rabinow, The Foucault Reader (1979).

Franssen, Maarten. "Design, use, and the physical and intentional aspects of technical artifacts." Philosophy and Design. Springer Netherlands, 2008. 21-35.

Fry, Tony. "Sacred Design I. A Re-creational Theory." R. Buchanan, R. & V. Margolin, V.(Eds.). Discovering design: explorations in design studies (1995): 190-218.

Gadamer, Hans-Georg. Truth and method. Continuum, 2004.

Gallagher, Shaun, and Dan Zahavi. The phenomenological mind. Routledge, 2012.

Galloway, Alexander R. The interface effect. Polity, 2012.

Gibson, James Jerome. The ecological approach to visual perception. Routledge, 1986.

Halpin, Harry, Andy Clark, and Michael Wheeler. "Towards a philosophy of the web: representation, enaction, collective intelligence." (2010)

Harman, Graham. The quadruple object. John Hunt Publishing, 2011.

Harman, Graham. Heidegger explained: From phenomenon to thing. Vol. 4. Open Court, 2013.

Harman, Graham. Tool-being: Heidegger and the metaphysics of objects. Open Court, 2013.

Harraway, Donna. "A cyborg manifesto: science, technology, and socialist-feminism in the late twentieth century." Simians, cyborgs and women: The reinvention of nature (1991): 149-181.

Heidegger, Martin. "The origin of the work of art (1936)." Basic Writings (1993): 139-212.

Heidegger, Martin. "The Thing, in "Poetry Language Thought." (1971): 184-5

Heidegger, Martin. What is called thinking?. Vol. 21. HarperCollins, 1976.

Heidegger, Martin. "Building dwelling thinking." Basic Writings. New York: Harper and Row, 1977.

Heidegger, Martin. The question concerning technology, and other essays. Harper Perennial, 1982.

Heidegger, Martin. The basic problems of phenomenology. Vol. 478. Indiana University Press, 1988.

Heidegger, Martin. Poetry, Language, Thought (Perennial Classics). Cidade: HarperCollins Publishers, 2001.

Heidegger, Martin. Being and time. HarperCollins, 2008.

Hookway, Branden. Interface. MIT Press, 2014.

Houkes, Wybo. "Designing is the construction of use plans." Philosophy and design. Springer Netherlands, 2008. 37-49.

Ihde, Don. Technics and praxis. Vol. 24. Dordrecht: Reidel, 1979.

Ihde, Don. Technology and the lifeworld: From garden to earth. No. 560. Indiana University Press, 1990.

Ihde, Don. Bodies in technology. Vol. 5. U of Minnesota Press, 2002.

Ihde, Don. "The designer fallacy and technological imagination." Philosophy and Design (2008): 51-59.

Ihde, Don. Postphenomenology and technoscience: The Peking university lectures. SUNY Press, 2009.

Ihde, Don. Heidegger's technologies: Postphenomenological perspectives. Fordham Univ Press, 2010.

Ingold, Tim. Making: Anthropology, archaeology, art and architecture. Routledge, 2013.

"Interview with Tim Berners-Lee." Impact Lab. 25 March 2006. 12 April 2014 <http://www.impactlab.net/2006/03/25/interview-with-tim-berners-lee/>

Johansson-Sköldberg, Ulla, Jill Woodilla, and Mehves Çetinkaya. "Design thinking: past, present and possible futures." Creativity and Innovation Management 22.2 (2013): 121-146.

Kimbell, Lucy. "Design practices in design thinking." European Academy of Management (2009): 1-24. (a)

Kimbell, Lucy. "Insights from Service Design Practice." 8th European Academy of Design Conference. 2009. (b)

Kiran, Asle H. "Technological presence: Actuality and potentiality in subject constitution." Human studies 35.1 (2012): 77-93.

Kolko, Jon. "Sensemaking and framing: A theoretical reflection on perspective in design synthesis." Design Research Society (2010) (a)

Kolko, Jon. "Abductive thinking and sensemaking: The drivers of design synthesis." Design Issues 26.1 (2010): 15-28. (b)

Krippendorff, Klaus. "On the essential contexts of artifacts or on the proposition that" design is making sense (of things)"." Design Issues (1989): 9-39.

Krippendorff, Klaus. The semantic turn: A new foundation for design. crc Press, 2004.

Lakoff, George, and Mark Johnson. Philosophy in the flesh: The embodied mind and its challenge to western thought. Basic books, 1999.

Lakoff, George, and Mark Johnson. Metaphors we live by. University of Chicago press, 2008.

Latour, Bruno. "Where are the missing masses? The sociology of a few mundane artifacts." (1992): 225-258.

Latour, Bruno. "On technical mediation." Common knowledge 3.2 (1994): 29-64.

Latour, Bruno. "A cautious Prometheus? A few steps toward a philosophy of design (with special attention to Peter Sloterdijk)." Proceedings of the 2008 annual international conference of the design history society. 2008.

Latour, Bruno. "Spheres and networks: two ways to reinterpret globalization." Harvard Design Magazine 30 (2009)

Lawson, Bryan. How designers think: the design process demystified. Routledge, 2006.

Martin, Roger L. The design of business: why design thinking is the next competitive advantage. Harvard Business Press, 2009.

May, Michael. "Beyond Affordances-Why direct perception is not enough in design engineering." Proceedings of CEPHAD 2010 Conference.(www.dkds.dk/Forskning/Projekter/CEPHAD). 2010.

Mitcham, Carl. "Dasein versus design: The problematics of turning making into thinking." International Journal of Technology and Design Education 11.1 (2001): 27-36.

Merleu-Ponty, Maurice. "Phenomenology of perception." Trans. Colin Smith. London: Routledge & Kegan Paul (1962).

Mitcham, Carl. "Dasein versus design: The problematics of turning making into thinking." International Journal of Technology and Design Education 11.1 (2001): 27-36.

Morozov, Evgeny. To save everything, click here: The folly of technological solutionism. PublicAffairs, 2013.

Nelson, Harold G., and Erik Stolterman. The design way: Intentional change in an unpredictable world: Foundations and fundamentals of design competence. Educational Technology, 2003.

Norman, Donald. "The design of everyday things." Doubled Currency, 1988.

Oosterling, Henk. "Dasein as design or: Must design save the world." Premselalecture 2009 (2009).

Preston, Beth. "The case of the recalcitrant prototype." Doing things with things: the design and use of everyday objects (2006): 15-27.

Ries, Eric. The lean startup: How today's entrepreneurs use continuous innovation to create radically successful businesses. Random House LLC, 2011.

Rittel, Horst WJ, and Melvin M. Webber. "Dilemmas in a general theory of planning." Policy sciences 4.2 (1973): 155-169.

Rowe, C. J., and Sarah Broadie, eds. Nicomachean ethics. Oxford University Press, 2002.

Rutsky, R. L. "High Techne: Art and Aesthetics from the Machine Age to the Posthuman." (1999).

De Saussure, Ferdinand. Course in general linguistics. Columbia University Press, 2011.

Schön, Donald A. The reflective practitioner: How professionals think in action. Vol. 5126. Basic books, 1983.

Secomandi, F. "Interface Matters: Postphenomenological perspectives on service design." (2012).

Simmel, Georg. "The handle." Georg Simmel 1918 (1858): 267-275.

Simon, Herbert Alexander. The sciences of the artificial. Vol. 136. MIT press, 1969.

Souza, Clarisse Sieckenius. The semiotic engineering of human-computer interaction. The MIT press, 2005.

Spool, Jared. "Design is the Rendering of Intent. " *UIE* 30 December 2013.   Web.   3   September   2014. <http://www.uie.com/articles/design_rendering_intent/>

Stiegler, Bernard. Technics and time: the fault of Epimetheus. Vol. 1. Stanford University Press, 1998.

Tonkinwise, Cameron. "Knowing by Being-There Making: Explicating the Tacit Post-Subject in Use." Studies in Material Thinking 1.2 (2008)

Tonkinwise, Cameron. "Lean Antinomies." Online video. Vimeo. Vimeo. 29. May. 2014. Web. 31. May. 2014.

Turner, Phil, Susan Turner, and Fiona Carroll. "The tourist gaze: Towards contextualised virtual environments." Spaces, spatiality and technology. Springer Netherlands, 2005. 281-297.

Verbeek, Peter-Paul. "Devices of engagement: on Borgmann's philosophy of information and technology." (2002)

Verbeek, Peter-Paul, and Petran Kockelkoren. "The things that matter." Design Issues 14.3 (1998)

Verbeek, Peter-Paul. "Artifacts and attachment: A post-script philosophy of mediation." (2005) (a)

Verbeek, Peter-Paul. What things do: Philosophical reflections on technology, agency, and design. Penn State Press, 2005 (b)

Verbeek, Peter-Paul. "Acting artifacts." User behavior and technology development. Springer Netherlands, 2006. 53-60.

Verbeek, Peter-Paul. "Cyborg intentionality: Rethinking the phenomenology of human–technology relations." Phenomenology and the Cognitive Sciences 7.3 (2008): 387-395.

Verbeek, Peter-Paul. "Expanding mediation theory." Foundations of science 17.4 (2012): 391-395.

Vermaas, P., Wybo Houkes, and Jeroen de Ridder. "A Philosophical Analysis of Designing." Design Research in the Netherlands, H. Achten, K. Dorst, PJ Stappers, B. de Vries, Editors, Eindhoven, ISBN (2005): 90-6814.)

Vermaas, Pieter E., and Wybo Houkes. "Use plans and artefact functions: An intentionalist approach to artefacts and their use." Doing things with things: The design and use of everyday objects (2006): 29-48.

Waddington, David I. "A field guide to Heidegger: Understanding 'the question concerning technology'." Educational Philosophy and Theory 37.4 (2005): 567-583.

Weiser, Mark, and John Seely Brown. "The coming age of calm technology." Beyond calculation. Springer New York, 1997. 75-85.

Wendt, Thomas. "Information Cartilage." Journal of Information Architecture. 5.1-2. 2013

Wendt, Thomas. "A Phenomenological Approach to Understanding Information and its Objects." Reframing Information Architecture. Springer International Publishing, 2014. 61-69. (a)

Wendt, Thomas. "Designing for Transparency and the Myth of the Modern Interface." UX *Magazine*. UX Magazine. 26 August 2013. 4 October 2014. <http://uxmag.com/articles/designing-for-transparency-and-the-myth-of-the-modern-> (b)

Willis, Anne-Marie. "Ontological designing." *Design philosophy papers* 4.2 (2006): 69-92.

Wimsatt, William K., and Monroe C. Beardsley. "The intentional fallacy." The Sewanee Review (1946): 468-488.

Winograd, Terry, and Fernando Flores. Understanding computers and cognition: A new foundation for design. Intellect Books, 1986.

Wittgenstein, Ludwig. Philosophical investigations. John Wiley & Sons, 2010.

Zaccai, Gianfranco. "Art and technology, aesthetics redefined." Discovering Design–Explorations in Design Studies (1995): 3-12.

Notes

[1]. Interview, 2006
[2]. Halpin, Clark, and Wheeler, 2006
[3]. Cross, 2006
[4]. Mitcham, 2001
[5]. Oosterling, 2009
[6]. Heidegger, 2008
[7]. ibid.
[8]. Turner, Turner, and Carroll, 2005
[9]. Lakoff and Johnson, 2008
[10]. Dourish, 2004
[11]. Stiegler, 1998
[12]. Oosterling, 2009
[13]. See Simon, 1969
[14]. Latour, 2009
[15]. Beckett, 1995
[16]. ibid
[17]. ibid
[18]. Descartes, 1998
[19]. Dreyfus, 2007
[20]. Heidegger, 1988
[21]. Heidegger, 1988
[22]. Dreyfus, 1991
[23]. Rowe and Broadie, 2002.
[24]. Ihde, 2009
[25]. Dourish, 2004
[26]. Beckett, 1995
[27]. Heidegger, 2008
[28]. Beckett, 1995
[29]. Tonkinwise, 2014
[30]. Turner, 2011
[31]. Dreyfus, 1991

32. Bonsiepe, 1999
33. Dreyfus, 1991
34. Krippendorff, 2004
35. ibid
36. ibid
37. Heidegger, 1982
38. ibid
39. Rutsky, 1999
40. ibid
41. Heidegger, 1982
42. Harman, 2011; Harman, 2013
43. Heidegger, 1982
44. Feenberg, 2003
45. Weiser, 1997
46. Heidegger, 1982
47. Krippendorff, 1989
48. ibid
49. Heidegger, 2008
50. Heidegger, 1988
51. Heidegger, 1971
52. ibid
53. ibid
54. Heidegger, 1977
55. Flusser, 2013
56. Buchanan, 1995
57. Cross, 2011
58. Buchanan, 1995
59. Heidegger, 1976
60. ibid
61. Derrida, 2011
62. Heidegger, 1976
63. Merleau-Ponty, 1962
64. ibid
65. Heidegger, 2008

66. ibid
67. Gallagher and Zahavi, 2012
68. Agosta, 2011
69. Cross, 2011
70. Mitcham, 2001
71. Fry, 1995
72. Mitcham, 2001
73. Zaccai, 1995
74. Fry, 1995
75. Heidegger, 2001
76. Cross, 2006
77. Cross, 2011
78. Kolko, 2010b
79. Tonkinwise, 2008
80. Rittel and Webber, 1973; Buchanan, 1992
81. Johansson-Sköldberg, Woodilla, and Çetinkaya, 2013
82. Schön, 1983
83. Rittel and Webber, 1973
84. Lawson, 2006
85. Cross, 2006; Cross, 2011
86. Krippendorff, 2004
87. Brown, 2009
88. Ries, 2011
89. Rittel and Webber, 1973
90. Dorst, 2006
91. Heidegger, 1936
92. Saussure, 2011
93. Schön, 1983
94. Rittel and Webber, 1973; Dorst, 2006; Dorst and Cross, 2001
95. Cross, 2011
96. ibid
97. Kiran, 2012
98. Martin, 2009
99. Rittel and Webber, 1973

[100]. Dorst, 2006
[101]. ibid
[102]. ibid
[103]. Morozov, 2013
[104]. Basalla, 1988
[105]. Nelson and Sloterman, 2003
[106]. Latour, 2008
[107]. Ihde, 2010
[108]. Verbeek, 2005b
[109]. ibid
[110]. ibid
[111]. Kimbell, 2009a
[112]. Heidegger, 1988
[113]. Saussure, 2011
[114]. Verbeek and Kockelkoren, 1998
[115]. Merleau-Ponty, 1962
[116]. Verbeek, 2005a
[117]. Verbeek's, 2005b
[118]. See Barthes, 1971
[119]. Verbeek, 2005b
[120]. Verbeek, 2012
[121]. Verbeek, 2005a
[122]. Cross, 2011
[123]. Latour, 1994
[124]. ibid
[125]. Verbeek, 2006
[126]. Latour,1992
[127]. Heidegger, 1977
[128]. Spool, 2013
[129]. Wimsatt and Beardsley, 1946
[130]. See Barthes, 1971; Foucault, 1979
[131]. See Barthes, 1971
[132]. Ihde, 2008
[133]. Gadamer, 2004

134. Verbeek, 2008
135. Franssen, 2008
136. Houkes, 2008
137. Verbeek, 2005a
138. Ihde, 2002
139. ibid
140. Baudrillard, 1996
141. Krippendorff, 2004
142. Flusser, 2013
143. Ingold, 2013
144. Vermaas, Houkes, and Ridder, 2005
145. Preston, 2006
146. Ingold, 2013
147. Vermaas and Houkes, 2006
148. Borakar, 2010
149. Heidegger, 2001
150. ibid
151. ibid
152. Folkamnn, 2013
153. Latour, 2008
154. Brown, 2001
155. Heidegger, 2001
156. ibid
157. Flusser, 2013
158. Clark, 1997
159. Dreyfus, 1992
160. Wendt, 2014b
161. Dourish, 2004
162. Dreyfus, 2007
163. Chemero, 2011; Clark, 2008
164. Merleau-Ponty, 1962
165. Bonsiepe, 1999
166. Flusser, 2013
167. Gibson, 1986

[168]. ibid
[169]. Simmel, 1918
[170]. ibid
[171]. Tonkinwise, 2008
[172]. Krippendorff, 2004
[173]. Dourish, 2001
[174]. Krippendorff, 1989
[175]. ibid
[176]. ibid
[177]. ibid
[178]. Krippendorff, 2004
[179]. Wittengstein, 2010; Austin, 1975
[180]. Krippendorff, 2004
[181]. Bonsiepe, 1999
[182]. Bonsiepe, 1999
[183]. Galloway, 2012
[184]. Bonsiepe, 1999
[185]. Simon, 1969
[186]. Hookway 2014
[187]. Krippendorff, 2004
[188]. ibid
[189]. Wendt, 2014b
[190]. Secomandi, 2012
[191]. May, 2010
[192]. ibid
[193]. Verbeek and Kockelkoren, 1998
[194]. Verbeek, 2012
[195]. Ihde, 1990
[196] Krippendorff, 2004
[197]. ibid
[198]. Kimbell, 2009b
[199]. Dunne and Raby, 2013
[200]. Brereton, 2011
[201]. Dourish, 2004

202. Dourish and Bell, 2011
203. Dourish, 2004
204. ibid
205. Folkmann, 2014

Printed in Great Britain
by Amazon.co.uk, Ltd.,
Marston Gate.